Contents

Introduction v

Foreword vii

Acknowledgements ix

Transition from Primary School to Secondary School 1

Career Guidance and Counselling 9
by Brian Mooney, *President of Institute of Guidance Counsellors*

The Transition Year Programme 33
by Brian Mooney, *President of Institute of Guidance Counsellors*

Homework & Studying 43
by Rory Mulvey, *Student Enrichment Services*

Junior Certificate Subjects 67

Leaving Certificate Subjects 93

Bullying 135

Adolescent Development 155
by Dr. David Carey, *Froebel College of Education, Dublin*

Hidden Disabilities that may emerge in Secondary School 165
by Dr. David Carey, *Froebel College of Education, Dublin*

The Underachieving Adolescent 175
by Dr. David Carey, *Froebel College of Education, Dublin*

The Leaving Certificate Vocational Programme 185

The Leaving Certificate Applied 193

The National Parents Council - Post Primary 199

Introduction

Following on from 'The Essential Parents Guide to the Primary School Years', this book has been written as a guide for parents, dealing with all of the issues that you are likely to face during the Secondary School years in Ireland. In order to ensure that your child realises his or her full potential at secondary school, the book aims to equip you with all of the relevant information needed to enable you to maximise your support.

The book focuses on some of the key issues facing students in secondary school today, providing relevant advice and information. The aim is to make the whole secondary school experience as fruitful, enjoyable and problem / crisis free as possible. The guide includes:

- Some pointers on making the **transition from Primary School** to Secondary School a little easier
- A brief description of each of **the major subjects** included in the Junior and Leaving Certificate exams
- A section on **Homework and Study Skills**, outlining how students can maximise their time and effectiveness and how we can help them
- An article on the whole area of **career guidance** / subject choices / counselling and so on
- Information on **bullying** and how to deal with it in secondary school
- An explanation of the **Transition Year** and what it entails
- A description of the **different types of Leaving Certificates** available
- A series of articles on dealing with adolescents:
  - o **Adolescent development**
  - o **Hidden disabilities** that can emerge in secondary school children
  - o **The underachieving adolescent**
- A description of the **National Parents Council** and its role

Foreword

Publishing 'The Essential Parents Guide to the Primary School Years' in 2003 was a bit of a leap in the dark for me. I had a good hunch that a book to help *parents* to get through primary school would prove popular. However, I was a little sceptical as to whether the same need would apply to a book for parents of secondary school students. Surely the curriculum is too complex to summarise; teenagers don't want their parents involved; the system is that bit more impersonal…there were plenty of reasons.

And yet here I am, writing the foreword of 'the sequel I thought would never happen'! What changed my mind? All of the above reasons in fact, plus the number of people who urged me to do it. The fact is that there is an even greater demand for a book which brings parents closer to the school system in secondary than primary. Communications with teenagers can become strained, there is far less direct contact with a secondary school for a parent and yet the desire amongst parents to help their children is stronger than ever. The stakes are higher, the pressure to perform and conform is greater and the amount of information available to parents about what actually goes on is pretty meagre.

While there is a huge focus on academic performance in the Irish Education system, it's very important to remember the other aspects of secondary school life; friendships, sports, social development and so on and I have tried to emphasise their importance too throughout the book. It would be no harm if your child was to read some of it too.

There are many books outlining all of the mistakes that we as parents make – this is not one of them. This book is about giving you the confidence to know your place and play your part in this crucial phase for your child.

I would recommend that you dip in and out of the book rather than read it in one go. Certain sections and articles are age-specific and may not be relevant, but I hope it will be a good reference as you progress through the secondary school years. I welcome your feedback greatly so please contact me as per the details below with any comments.

Finally, I would like thank my wife Hilary, family and friends for their ongoing cheering and encouragement and want to dedicate this book to my three little supporters, Anna May, Tim and John.

Brian Gilsenan
July 2004

PrimaryABC
Abercorn House
57 Charleston Road
Ranelagh
Dublin 6
(01) 269 5008
primaryabc@eircom.net
www.primaryabc.ie

Acknowledgements

A book like this would be impossible to complete without the assistance and interest of some key people. I was fortunate to have received fantastic encouragement, help and contributions from three such professionals and I would like to thank them sincerely.

Dr. David Carey is Coordinator of Special Education at Froebel College of Education in Dublin.

Mr. Brian Mooney is the President of the Institute of Guidance Counsellors in Ireland. He also write a weekly article in The Irish Times on related subjects

Mr. Rory Mulvey is founder of Student Enrichment Services in Dublin, who provide courses on study techniques for students in over 300 schools nationwide every year.

I would also like to thank the many teachers who were kind enough to give me the benefit of their experience. Clodagh Lynch, who was very helpful for the Transition from Primary to Secondary article, Bobby Byrne, Brian Wall, Mark Hurley, Andy Carroll and Rosemary Mitchell.

Particular mention and thanks to Tommy Casserly (SES) for his great work on synopsising the subjects into manageable sections!

For the National Parents Council Post Primary, I'd like to thank Eleanor Petrie, Geraldine Perkins and particularly Valerie Burke for their help and encouragement.

Thanks to all involved in the Cool School Programme at the North Eastern Health Board, especially Deborah James. Thanks too to Sheila O'Driscoll from LCA and both Frances Holohan and Esther Herlihy from LCVP.

Final words of gratitude to Lynn Nalty for the great illustrations (again!) and to Frank Kearney at Keystrokes for his professionalism and patience.

THE TRANSITION
FROM
PRIMARY SCHOOL
TO
SECONDARY SCHOOL

The Transition from Primary School to Secondary School

The transition from primary school to secondary school is one of those life events that most people can recall in some way or other. In the main, it's a fairly manageable period and one that parents often get more emotional about than their children. The fact is that most children are more than ready for the step up to Secondary school. They will know people who already attend and are bound to know some who are about to join. The purpose of this article is to outline the major issues involved so that the experience can be facilitated and undertaken with minimum stress - for the whole family!

Big fish to small fish

By the time children reach their final years in primary school, they will be totally familiar with their school environment. They'll know their teacher very well, be comfortable with most if not all of the people in their class and will probably know most of the other faces in the school too. By sixth class, they are the most senior people in their school, they will be used to being given responsibility and they tend to be looked up to by the younger boys and girls in the school.

But within the space of two short months, September 1st sees these same students revert to being the most junior again in a brand new environment in a different location, with a different smell and atmosphere. Change can be a daunting prospect for any one of us but when you are 12 or 13 – with so many other 'complications' in your life - it is a change that takes quite a lot of adjustment.

The important thing to constantly remind yourself is that children and teenagers are more resilient and adaptable than we are (or give them credit for). Remember too that within a few short weeks, their new surroundings become more familiar and they'll be running from the PE Hall to the Science Lab and on to the Art room without the slightest stumble. The first couple of weeks can be traumatic though and this section offers both parent and child a survival plan to make the transition as smooth as possible.

Constant routine becomes constant change

The biggest change when entering the secondary school system is probably the constant change in the day-to-day routine. In primary school, there was one teacher all day in the one classroom. In Secondary school however, that routine changes utterly. There is a subject change every forty minutes approximately, and with this subject change there is a change of teacher. It is not unusual for a student to encounter eight or nine different teachers during a typical school day. A tip to help your child cope with this in the first few days is to advise them to write down the name of each new teacher beside the name of the subject.

Some subject changes will involve a change of classroom too and the second big change that the new first years have to cope with is the constant movement between classrooms throughout the day. Getting lost during the first few weeks will be inevitable for some. A good tip is to advise your child to always stay with at least one other person from the class...there is definitely safety and confidence in numbers!

All of this 'new-ness' is bound to have some effect on the student and in these early days of adjusting, parents should try to be supportive, understanding and encouraging, ensuring their child eats well and gets plenty of rest and 'down time'.

Number of subjects

Another big adjustment is the number of specific subjects your child will be covering. Depending on the school and the subject-choice structure, students in first year can cover anything up to fifteen different subjects (some will only be by way of introduction, to help students to select the subjects they wish to take for the Junior Cert.). Many of these are new and unfamiliar. An example of a typical timetable is included here, to give you an idea of what a typical day might look like.

Sample first year timetable

Time	Monday	Tuesday	Wednesday	Thursday	Friday
9:00	History	Maths	English	Geography	Religion
9:40	Irish	C.S.P.E.*	S.P.H.E.**	Maths	Science
10:20	**B**	**R**	**E**	**A**	**K**
10:40	Music	Irish	History	Art	Geography
11:20	Business	Science	Maths	French	German
12:00	PE	Religion	Careers	English	Business
12:40	**L**	**U**	**N**	**C**	**H**
1:30	Maths	Business	Computers	Science	Maths
2:10	Art	Music	French	Irish	English
2:50	Geography	English	Art	Music	PE

*C.S.P.E.: Civic, Social and Political Education
**S.P.H.E.: Social, Personal and Health Education

As you can see from the diversity, it is important at an early stage to help your child to develop a methodical approach to learning. Discuss all the subjects at home. Getting your child to explain what they have learnt so far in a particular subject will have two beneficial effects. It will help you to better understand a subject and getting your child to summarise a subject will also help to highlight, in their mind, how they are coping with it.

It is important to try to encourage a balance between all subjects. Everyone will have their own favourites and will excel at certain subjects. The problem is that neglecting a subject in the early stages – due to its perceived difficulty or maybe a personality clash with a teacher - may have an impact on subject choices in future years. Taking an early dislike to science and dropping it after first year or the Junior Cert. might limit the career choices available come fifth year. Certain third level courses require at least one science subject for example so be careful when it comes to choosing or dropping subjects. Take a look at the Career Guidance section on *page 9* and be sure that you or your child (preferably both) talk to the career guidance counsellor / principal regarding subject selections.

The Schoolbag

Their timetable will take a lot of getting used to. Part of this new routine will involve the organisation of the schoolbag before each day. It's a new skill that some may struggle with and a little help in the early days will ensure they have the right books, and the right homework on the right day!

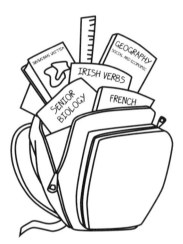

Homework

Homework time is obviously going to increase and with it comes several new adjustments from the Primary School homework routine. Not all subjects are covered every day and not all subjects involve homework. This may mean that your child has two hours homework on one night and maybe one hour the next night. One of the best skills you can help your child to learn is that of effective time management. Help your child to even out their homework pattern by encouraging them to develop a homework timetable. Certain subjects get homework nightly (Maths), others on every other day, others still on a weekly basis (Irish essay). Help them to devise a method to spread out the workload over the five nights of the week. Don't underestimate the importance of getting a structure and a sense of organisation at an early stage of their secondary school lives. Learning how to successfully manage their time is an invaluable life skill and will make the transition into their new environment a whole lot easier. See chapter on study skills, *page 43*.

School Reports

A new experience in secondary school is the regular reports that come home from the school. Aside from the exam reports, most schools have a regular report that must be signed by the parent. It will usually have an overall performance mark for each subject and space for any comments from any of the teachers. It might include the number of days absent or late and any general notes relating to your child's performance. Again, these should be monitored and taken seriously, particularly in first year. It is important that your child sees you as an extension of the school system – if you're dismissive of feedback from the school, it allows a negative attitude to develop in your child which is not in anyone's interest. If you have an issue you would like to discuss with a teacher or the principal, it is best done without the involvement of your child, in the initial instance anyway.

Extra-curricular activities:

Taking part in after-school activities is a great way of getting to know more students in the school. Whether it's in the drama circle, the computer club or on the playing field, each student should seek out activities which they enjoy. Taking part in such activities builds confidence, they get to mix with

other students from other years and as a result, they settle into the school environment more quickly. Students should be encouraged, from both home and school, to try out new activities. Whether they have tried something before or not, or even if they don't know what a particular activity entails, students should be encouraged to try practically everything available through the school.

Support Network

As stated, most children take the transition from primary school to secondary school in their stride. Schools have generally recognised the potential difficulties and have a good support network in place for first years. Most schools operate the system of the 'year head' (a teacher who has specific responsibility for the entire year). Many schools also appoint class 'tutors', 'mentors' and sixth year 'buddies' or 'prefects' who have the task of making the introduction to the school as pleasant and as painless as possible.

As parents, we can often feel a little helpless – our role is to be supportive, interested and encouraging. If you have any concerns about your child, the advice is to make contact with the school.

Take heart!

Finally, with all the ups and downs of the first few weeks, rest assured that by the time Sept 1st comes round again the following year, your child will enter the establishment as if they've been there forever. They will laugh at the new first years for getting lost, again, and will boss them around with all the authority that only a second year student can assume!

CAREER GUIDANCE AND COUNSELLING

By Brian Mooney,

President of the Institute of Guidance Counsellors

Career Guidance and Counselling

Pre-entry Guidance and Counselling

The Guidance and Counselling service at second level starts before the student enters the system. Guidance Counsellors work with the Principal, sixth class teachers and learning support teachers in feeder primary schools in order to identify children who might be in need of special needs or remedial support at second level. It is very important that any parent whose child is in receipt of any form of educational support in primary school communicates this information to the secondary school that their child is applying to. Currently many parents are reluctant to do this, as they fear that it might militate against their child's chances of being accepted into the school in question. I would question whether you would want your child in such a school? What would be the advantage of being in a school where your child's needs were not being catered for? Surely it is better to be totally honest with the schools in your area. In this way you will locate the schools that have developed good resources in the field of learning support and special needs. They will be more than anxious to put in place an educational plan for your child.

There can be controversy regarding the use of assessment tests, used by second level schools on proposed incoming pupils. From a Guidance Counsellor's perspective, these instruments are essential tools in identifying children who will need remedial support at second level. They should only be used for this purpose and no other. Any school that would use such a test to exclude a child is acting in a manner totally contrary to the Department of Education and Science regulations in this matter. They are also acting in a manner that is both ethically and morally bankrupt.

The Nature of the Irish Guidance and Counselling service

On entry to second level, every child is entitled to appropriate Guidance and Counselling to assist them in their educational and career choices, as outlined under sections 9 (c) & 9 (d) of the 1998 Education Act. This holistic service is delivered by and through Guidance Counsellors, who provide personal, social, educational and career guidance in all schools in Ireland.

No human being, be they child or adult, experiences life in a one-dimensional sense. All our actions, thoughts, feelings, and decisions are affected by our personal, social, educational and career experiences. Because every child in school (or adult in the wider world) is multi-dimensional, dealing with his or her educational and career decision-making processes requires an understanding on the part of the Guidance Counsellor of the personal and social circumstances of that child.

In our schools, Guidance Counsellors work with children to help them:

- Develop and accept a whole picture of their talents and abilities
- To grow in independence and develop their ability to take responsibility for themselves
- To make well informed choices about their lives and to assist them to follow through on those choices.

Because of the rapidly changing nature of Irish society, many children live in difficult social circumstances. The problems that children experience in their personal lives are many and varied.

(a) **Crime Problems.** Addictions to drugs or alcohol, vandalism, petty theft

(b) **Emotional Problems.** Anger management, bereavement, chronic shyness, depression, issues of low self esteem, suicidal thoughts and tendencies

(c) **Home Problems.** Family poverty, homelessness, separation anxiety, adoption maladjustment

(d) **Health Problems.** Eating disorders, issues around body image during periods of rapid hormonal change

(e) **Sexual Problems.** Issues of sexual abuse, sexual identity, pregnancy, rape, abortion, relationship issues

(f) **School Problems.** Authority issues, bullying, peer relationships, career choice confusion, stress, examination fears and failures, making friends, motivation, school refusal, school retention, issues of race or ethnicity, learning difficulties

It is for all of these reasons that the service available in schools has to be much more than a careers service. Nobody, be they child or adult, can effectively deal with educational and career issues in their lives without first coming to terms with, and developing mechanisms to deal with, issues causing major personal and social difficulties in their lives. That is why the Irish service is a Guidance and Counselling service, staffed by professionally trained Guidance Counsellors, who have a full post graduate qualification in Guidance and Counselling.

The nature of the support that Guidance Counsellors provide to the personal and social development of children in schools is determined by the allocation of Guidance Counselling resources provided by the board of management, from within the resources allocated by the Department of Education and Science. As well as being provided on a one to one basis in the Guidance Counsellors office, these services are also available through various programmes throughout the rest of the school's curriculum. These include SPHE (Social Personal Health Education), Religious Education, Relationship and Sexuality Education and Pastoral

Guidance & Counselling

Care programmes. Many schools also have the services of a Home School Liaison Service, whose members visit the homes of children experiencing difficulties in school.

What does the Guidance and Counselling service hope to provide students with, through personal and social support?

(1) To develop skills in a range of areas crucial to their educational and career development. These would include the skills of:

- Self-management of their time, to achieve their educational goals
- Self-understanding, to enable them to evaluate the options and opportunities available to them
- Belonging and integrating within their school peer group, and other peer groups
- Communication skills, to enable them to accurately articulate themselves, either verbally or in writing.

(2) To recognise their own talents and achievements and identify their strengths and weaknesses.

(3) To develop coping strategies to deal with stress, personal and social issues, and the challenges posed by adolescence and adulthood.

(4) To develop interpersonal skills and awareness of the needs of others.

(5) To establish good patterns of decision-making and learn how to make informed choices.

(6) To learn how to make successful transitions from junior to senior cycle; from Post Primary to higher education or on to employment.

The level, intensity and duration of the counselling provided by professional Guidance Counsellors in schools depends on the seriousness of the difficulties encountered. There are limits to both the professional competence and the appropriateness of what can be dealt with in a school Guidance and Counselling service. Where it becomes obvious that a child needs the services of a psychotherapist, Guidance Counsellors make referrals to appropriate services, either through the health board or the family doctor.

Where the difficulty is one of educational disability, the Guidance Counsellor will seek the support of an educational psychologist through the National Educational Psychological Service. Due to the limited nature of the service available in many schools from NEPS, parents often find it necessary to have their child seen privately by an educational psychologist, where problems in this area are identified in schools. Recent changes announced by the Department of Education and Science to provide all schools with access to locally appointed Special Education Needs Organisers who will have the responsibility to allocate resources to schools in accordance with their needs, should help, in time, to alleviate the difficulties in this area.

The nature of the <u>Educational</u> Guidance Service

Guidance counsellors give students and their parents clear concise information concerning the subjects available in the school. This includes information on the implications and consequences of choosing or not choosing particular subjects or their level, i.e. ordinary or higher, for future course or career choice. They provide students with an opportunity to explore their interests and subject choices and help them see the links between them and career areas. They assist parents and students in making informed choices from among the various programmes available in the school: Junior Certificate Programme, Transition Year Programme, Leaving Certificate Programme, Leaving Certificate Vocational Programme, Leaving Certificate Applied Programme. See *pages 185, 193* for a description of the last two.

Guidance Counsellors also assist students in identifying their own most effective learning styles, helping them to develop effective study patterns, note-taking skills, examination techniques and time management skills. These time management skills enable students to effectively organise their time throughout the week between the demands of school, work and leisure activities, as well as understanding the time commitment required to successfully achieve their potential in the state examination system See the article on study skills on *page 43.*

Given the wide range of subjects taken in second level schools and the diversity of teaching styles encountered by students in any one day, it is not surprising that students often need the support of the Guidance and Counselling service to cope with such diversity.

The nature of the <u>Career</u> Guidance Service

At the heart of the Guidance and Counselling system is the career guidance service. Students are provided with an objective assessment of their aptitudes, through the administration and interpretation of Differential Aptitude Tests. They are also provided with an objective assessment of their achievements through an evaluation of the results of their performance in all aspects of school life, both academically and extra curricular.

The core of a Guidance Counsellor's work in the area of careers is to provide students with a comprehensive understanding of the educational, vocational and career options available to them. This will include information on the career progression routes and lifelong learning opportunities available to them. Parents can often be very conservative in the career option they wish to consider for their children, often falling back on their own experiences at that age. It is the job of the Guidance Counsellor, supported by agencies such as FAS, to inform both parents and students of the constantly growing range of career opportunities available in the economy today. The ultimate aim of the Career Guidance Programme is to facilitate students in developing individual career plans, based on their achievements, interests and subject choices.

Information Communication Technology in Career Guidance

The role of Information Communication Technology skills in career exploration and planning is of paramount importance to all those investigating their career options today. All schools have computer facilities, although many students find it difficult to access such facilities due to limited timetabling opportunities during school time. The computer and the Internet are becoming the medium of communication of information for everyone today. The role of the Guidance Counsellor is to assist students in identifying appropriate sites to visit during their career exploration work. The problem for all users of the world wide web today is in identifying quality information from among the vast volumes available online.

The Institute of Guidance Counsellors and the Department of Education and Science jointly produce the most important ICT resource available to students. It is produced in CD-Rom format and is also available online at **www.qualifax.ie**. It contains up to date information on everything that a prospective student might require when choosing courses after the completion of the Leaving Certificate. It contains the entire course details of every Post Leaving Certificate, Higher National Certificate,  Ordinary Degree, and Higher Degree available in the island of Ireland. It also contains details of courses available through FAS, Fáilte Ireland and many other course providers. In addition, it contains a module on Government financial support available through the grants system, a resource library of useful reference texts, a subject definitions module to enable prospective students to understand what particular course titles actually mean and details on educational opportunities in other EU countries. The programme includes an 'interest inventory' to enable students to get an initial insight into their possible career interests, plus a search engine to enable users to refine down the volume of courses to be explored. To cut down on the costs of using the service online, the programme is made available to students and parents in a CD-Rom format through the Guidance Counsellor in schools. Tens of thousands of copies of the programme are distributed for home use each year.

Guidance & Counselling

Additionally, FAS produces a programme in CD-Rom format called **Career Directions**, which contains information on a wide range of career opportunities. It is an extremely useful resource and can be acquired through FAS offices nationwide. It is also available on the Qualifax CD-Rom.

Another extremely useful IT resource is a programme called **Careers World**, which is produced by Woodgrange Technologies. It is available through the Guidance programme in all schools. It contains details regarding 134 'real life' jobs in 22 of Ireland's major employers in both the public and private sector, including video clips of 65 people doing these jobs. The programme has a self-exploration 'Preference Exercise' tool, which helps users discover their strengths and weaknesses. It also provides information on 29 industry sectors and the people who work in them. Finally it has a very useful module on improving study techniques and memory skills. For further information visit the Careers World web site at **www.careersworld.com**.

In recent years there has been much concern regarding the reduced numbers of students taking science subjects at Leaving Certificate level. Forfas, through the Expert Group on Future Skills Needs has recently produced a very useful CD-Rom for schools, entitled **'Up2u'**, containing everything students need to explore careers in science, technology and engineering. It provides a guide to the science and technology subjects available at Leaving Certificate level, including students describing their own project work in science and technology, and explanations on what is involved. It also profiles dozens of career options in the field of science and technology from people who actually work in these areas.

Apart from CD-Rom programmes, all colleges in Ireland offering courses to students have web sites, setting out full details of their courses and the facilities available on campus. The same applies to industry bodies and professional associations representing all career areas. Students are encouraged as part of their Career Guidance investigations to explore these options fully. One method of doing this is a career investigation undertaken as part of a Transition Year of Leaving Certificate Vocational Programme. See chapter on 'Transition Year', *page 33*.

Guidance in <u>First Year</u> of Secondary School

On entering a secondary school the first emotion most students experience is one of excitement tinged with anticipation and a little apprehension. Moving from an environment where you are the tallest and undisputed senior student, to being the smallest and most junior, is not without its difficulties. There is an entire chapter devoted to this topic, see *page 1*.

The entire school staff attempts to make this transition as smooth as possible for all students and the role of the Guidance Counsellor is central to this process. They will have met parents prior to the child entering the school to explain to them the nature of the guidance service provided, across the areas already mentioned, namely personal, social, educational and careers.

In most schools, students do not have to make choices from among a menu of subjects until they have had a chance to sample them all in first year, although a handful of schools insist on such choices being made on entry. I believe such a policy is educationally unsound, as students or parents should not be expected to make choices when they have not yet had an opportunity to take the subject for a year. Apart from a tiny minority of schools, students study a wide range of subjects in first year and are asked to make choices from among a range of optional subjects thereafter. All students take core subjects at Junior Certificate level, including Irish (unless exempted because of educational disability or being over the age of twelve on entry into the Irish Education system), English, Maths, History, Geography, Religion and PE. A large majority of students also take Science, and a Continental Language. Other subjects available to students include Business, Technology, Mechanical Drawing, Music, Art, and a range of practical subjects. There is a brief description of each subject from *page 67*.

A key role of the Guidance Counsellor is to ensure that the parent and student are fully aware of the third level/career implications of particular subject choices. Decisions taken at the end of first year can and do have long-term implications for the availability of career and course options later on.

A few examples will help explain the issues:
- Students opting for ordinary level Irish are excluded from pursuing Primary School teaching through the Irish training Colleges
- Students opting for ordinary level Maths are not going to be able to enter directly into an Engineering Degree programme.
- Students who do not take a Continental Language are excluded from entry to National University of Ireland Colleges. An exception to this rule is Trinity College, who will accept Irish as a second language alongside English.

Thus, subjects choices made at the end of first year are crucial to career choice later on and the Guidance programme should ensure that all involved are aware of the long-term implications of their options.

Apart from subject choice, the first year Guidance programme will help students come to terms with the study and homework requirements of a new curriculum. It is a major shock to students to find themselves dealing with over a dozen teachers, with different teaching styles and homework requirements (instead of one teacher at Primary level). The Guidance Counsellor normally gives a number of classes to first year students to help them develop strategies to deal with this change. Most students very quickly come to terms with their new environment, but there are always a small number who find this transition difficult, and the Guidance Counsellor and or Year Head can work with such students to help them settle down successfully in secondary school. (See chapter on 'Transition from primary school', *page 1*).

Special Needs

Sometimes students manifest behavioural difficulties in first year that come to the attention of the Guidance Counsellor. These can often be attributed to undiagnosed or unreported educational disabilities, which were not detected in Primary school or were not reported by parents, for fear of the child not getting a place in their 'preferred' school. The Guidance Counsellor will normally meet with such students and carry out a series of assessment instruments to ascertain the nature of the problem. They may seek the assistance of an educational psychologist from NEPS. If the student is deemed to suffer from a severe learning difficulty, the psychologist will recommend a number of hours of one to one support from a special needs teacher. The Dept. of Education and Science normally approves this recommendation, but it can take time to work its way through the system. The recent announcement of the appointment of Special Education Needs Organisers should alleviate this problem.

Sometimes the difficulties manifested by students in school in first year are a reflection of difficulties in the home environment. For some children, school is a secure environment compared to their experience at home. This is a sad reflection of the ills of society and can put huge demands on schools that they were never designed to handle. In many cases, schools manage to provide enough support to enable students to survive in the system, often I may say at huge cost to staff and fellow students. Sadly, many other students begin to drift away from the school system and drop out before they take the Junior Certificate. Guidance Counsellors, alongside Year Heads and Home School Liaison teachers attempt to help such students find the motivation to persevere in school, usually through one-to-one support. (See articles by *Dr. David Carey from pages 155*).

Guidance in <u>Second</u> and <u>Third Year</u> in Secondary School

It is very rare in Irish schools for Guidance Counsellors to have timetabled weekly class contact with students in second and third year, unless it is through a Social Personal and Health Education class or a Civics, Social and Political Education class. Where such contact exists, students may begin to explore the broad career areas. A good programme will encourage students to consider a wide range of educational and career choices, not bound by traditional considerations of gender or social stereotyping. Students can also be provided with information on the competencies and skills required for the world of work today, including the skills necessary to secure and retain employment. It is usually far too early to begin to focus on specific roles within career areas, but as students personalities mature it is possible to begin to see the general areas of interest that students are beginning to gravitate towards.

The role of the Guidance Counsellor for second and third year students is mainly a supporting one, helping to develop good study and examination techniques. They will help them to develop an awareness of the implications of the subjects they will select for the Leaving Certificate programme on future college course and career choice. Guidance Counsellors also play a central role in outlining to both parents and third year students the short and long term benefits of taking the Transition year programme. See chapter on 'Transition Year' *page 33.*

Guidance at Senior Cycle (<u>Fourth Year</u> to <u>Sixth Year</u>)

A major issue of concern to Guidance Counsellors is that fifteen percent of students do not enter the senior cycle. The loss of students to the system starts with the transfer from primary to second level when approximately a thousand students each year fail to transfer. The latest

Census figures show us that this trend continues throughout second level with boys being the main casualties. These figures show that the number of boys in full time education at 18 years of age is currently 60%, with the corresponding figure for girls being 75%.

For the students who do enter senior cycle, a growing proportion of them take a three-year programme, comprising of Transition Year and a two-year Leaving Certificate programme. Up to this point, there has been no timetabled activity for Career Guidance and Counselling; Guidance Counsellors acquired class contact with students by borrowing a class period from a colleague. Because of its increased importance in the senior cycle, the majority of students have a single class period timetabled with their Guidance Counsellor each week. This enables the Guidance Counsellor to design a comprehensive programme of work to ensure that all students make the appropriate choices for themselves in the area of career and college choices.

Career guidance at senior cycle has three emphases:

- Stimulating career development
- Providing the forum for exploration and discussion
- Aiding placement

The Guidance Counsellor helps students to:

1. Explore their attitudes to further education, training and employment.
2. Manage the transition from post-primary to further or higher education, training or employment.
3. Develop their ICT skills of research so that they can be self-directed in their career exploration and development.
4. Learn about job search and job retention skills, especially in the context of students taking the Leaving Certificate Applied and the Leaving Certificate Vocational Programme (see *pages 185 and 193*).
5. Learn about the world of work, including employment rights and responsibilities.

6. Acquire and understand information about further and higher education and training courses, including course content, workload and progression routes.

7. Acquire and understand information prepared by public bodies, public agencies and employers regarding career opportunities.

8. Make contact and develop linkages with colleges of further and higher education and training organisations to help them make their decisions regarding course and college choices.

9. Have opportunities to attend events such as college open days, career fairs, and visits by and to employers

10. Understand the reality of working life in particular careers through presentations by past pupils and parents on their career area.

11. Differentiate between the career expectations they are beginning to develop for themselves as compared to the expectations that parents may hold for them.

12. Acquire ways to identify careers that match those identified for them through psychometric instruments and other means of research, and are in line with their interests and aptitudes.

13. Acquire the skills to perform effectively in interviews through the organisation of mock interviews, usually through a panel of parents/past pupils

14. Understand the nature of the financial supports that may be available through the grants system to enable them to finance themselves through college.

Transition Year (see also *page 33*)

Transition Year is the stage where students engage with the world of work through work experience. For some, this work experience may form part of their career exploration but for most, it is simply an extension of part time working they may already be involved in. To enhance the value of the work experience, students in Transition year are required to keep a daily log of their work experience and to write a review of the benefits that they think they gained from it. This process is critical to its usefulness in developing student's insights into the reality of working life.

They will also be introduced to the development and production of their CV and the skills involved in writing a letter of introduction to a potential employer in Transition Year.

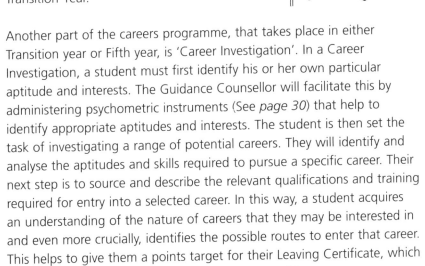

Another part of the careers programme, that takes place in either Transition year or Fifth year, is 'Career Investigation'. In a Career Investigation, a student must first identify his or her own particular aptitude and interests. The Guidance Counsellor will facilitate this by administering psychometric instruments (See *page 30*) that help to identify appropriate aptitudes and interests. The student is then set the task of investigating a range of potential careers. They will identify and analyse the aptitudes and skills required to pursue a specific career. Their next step is to source and describe the relevant qualifications and training required for entry into a selected career. In this way, a student acquires an understanding of the nature of careers that they may be interested in and even more crucially, identifies the possible routes to enter that career. This helps to give them a points target for their Leaving Certificate, which is an important element in student motivation and focus.

Fifth Year

Fifth year is the most intense year from a career guidance point of view. Guidance Counsellors, through weekly classes, cover a large proportion of the fourteen-point programme outlined above. They seek to equip the students to make the appropriate choices for themselves and much use is made of the computer room, where the vast range of ICT resources will be explored.

Students gradually develop an understanding of all aspects of further and higher education, progression routes, the labour market, possible financial supports and a myriad of other issues relevant to their future careers and options.

Sixth Year

Sixth year is when final decisions have to be made regarding career progression. The Guidance year starts for many students with a visit to the Irish Times/Institute of Guidance Counsellors 'Higher Options Exhibition' in the RDS in Dublin. Over twenty five thousand Leaving Certificate students visit this exhibition each year. Every college in Ireland, plus numerous colleges from the UK and further afield attend. Students also receive a series of lectures on all aspects of college entry, including a detailed one from the CAO on the Irish third level application system. Similar exhibitions, on a smaller scale, are organised by regional branches of the Institute of Guidance Counsellors throughout Ireland.

Many third level and further education colleges visit schools to make presentations to sixth years between September and January each year to highlight the benefits of attending their particular college or faculty.

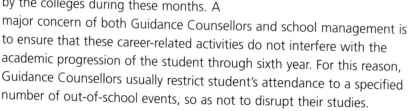

These visits are very professional, usually involving a thirty-minute presentation. Students also attend Open Days laid on by the colleges during these months. A major concern of both Guidance Counsellors and school management is to ensure that these career-related activities do not interfere with the academic progression of the student through sixth year. For this reason, Guidance Counsellors usually restrict student's attendance to a specified number of out-of-school events, so as not to disrupt their studies.

Application Systems

The ultimate aim of the Guidance and Counselling service is to put the student in a position to make a successful application to a college, a training place or employment of their choice on leaving second level education. The vast majority of sixth year students apply to the CAO for a place on a Higher Certificate, Ordinary Degree, or Higher Degree course in the Republic of Ireland. They have ten choices on their Higher Certificate/Ordinary Degree list and ten on their Higher Degree list.

Entry to each course is governed by three criteria:

1. college entry requirements
2. course entry requirements
3. points

The order of these criteria is important. Students sometimes forget the first two requirements and then cannot understand why a place has not been offered to them, when they have achieved more points than the minimum published in the newspapers for that course. The reason is they have not the appropriate subjects, at the minimum level or grade for entry to that course.

Once a student meets the first two requirements, he/she is placed on a list of applicants which is then dealt with in order of points achievement.

The CAO form

Parents often ask my advice directly and through my Irish Times column on how to fill in the CAO form. My advice is as follows:

- Apply for the courses you want, in the order that you want them, ensuring that you are taking the appropriate subjects as laid out by the college
- Never apply for a course if you have not read the entire syllabus. The biggest cause of third level dropout is a lack of understanding of the subjects within a course option

- Apply online. The online system will not allow you to make many simple errors which can occur on the paper form. It is also cheaper.

Tens of thousands of students take Post Leaving Certificate courses in Vocational Education Committee schools. Most of these courses are practical in nature and of one year duration, leading directly to employment. Every year over two thousand reserved places are awarded to PLC graduates in courses allocated by the CAO. In this way for instance, a student who applied for a place on a nursing degree programme, but failed to secure the points for entry, could take a one-year PLC course. Provided they secure five distinctions in their FETAC (NCVA level 2) course, including a distinction in a specific module, they can then apply for one of a small number of places reserved for PLC graduates, on their original Degree choice.

As can be seen from the above example, a ladder system operates at further and higher education and the entire thrust of both Government and colleges policy is to support and encourage as many students as possible to progress to the upper limit of their potential through the education system.

Northern Ireland and UK

Because of the geographic location of a number of further and third level colleges in Northern Ireland, it is often more convenient for students living in border regions to apply through the UCAS UK system to college. This system differs from the Irish system in that a student can make up to six course applications, each one of equal rank. The applications will be passed on to the individual colleges and each one will evaluate the application. This often involves an interview in the college, in the springtime of the year of entry, so travel becomes a factor. Following this process, the college may offer a place to a student, specifying the minimum grades they will have to achieve in their individual subjects in the Leaving Certificate. Depending on their Leaving Certificate results, a student may have a number of courses to choose from. UCAS also operates a 'clearing system', where college places not taken up in the first phase are offered to students who initially failed to secure a place. To all intents and purposes this process is an auction. Apart from students in border regions, a small number of Irish students also choose to study on the British mainland, particularly in a course that has restricted numbers of places on offer in Ireland.

Training and Employment

Apart from college options, many students take up places in apprenticeships after completing their Leaving Certificate. Students must secure an employer who is prepared to offer them an apprenticeship. Only at that stage can they register with FAS for training. There are many in Guidance and Counselling, including myself, who feel that this is a highly inefficient system. Would it not be more appropriate for a student to apply to FAS initially and have FAS act as a clearinghouse for employers seeking trainee apprenticeships? This system operates in a number of EU countries.

Be that as it may, once a student is registered with an employer, they enter into a seven phase training programme. Three phases are 'off the job', in a FAS training centre and four are 'on the job' with the employer. The process normally takes three years. At the end of that process, the student is awarded their qualification, which is recognised throughout the EU.

Finally, there are thousands of high quality opportunities for students in employment, following successful completion of their Leaving Certificate. Fáilte Ireland has thousands of terrific career opportunities in the Hotel and Catering industry, servicing our tourist market. The public services, through the Civil Service Commission, the Gardaí, the Defence Forces and the Local Authorities all offer excellent employment opportunities for students. Business and Industry also seek schoolleavers to service the growing needs of our dynamic economy. The message to all students is to stay in the education system until Leaving Certificate if at all possible. The opportunities, which the Guidance and Counselling service can help you to access, are many and varied.

The use of Psychometric Instruments in Career Guidance

There is much discussion in educational circles as to the usefulness of psychometric instruments in clarifying career choice. Such instruments measure General Ability, Aptitude, Occupational Interest, and Personality. Parents can often be very concerned about the results of such assessments as students can be 'labelled' as a result of a test taken in school. As a practising Guidance Counsellor, I find psychometric instruments very useful tools in conjunction with a wide range of other factors in helping me assess a student's possible career options. They should never be considered on their own, as a measure of students' potential.

General Ability Instruments
General ability tests measure intelligence. Intelligence is not directly observable but can be deducted or inferred from the behaviour of people. General ability instruments measure intelligence by presenting a wide variety of tasks to a group of students or an individual student. Such tests cover items such as vocabulary, arithmetic, spatial skills, in increasing order of difficulty. A student's performance is measured against that of a similar group of his or her own age and is reported back in the form of an IQ score.

Aptitude Instruments
These come in two forms, individual and group. Generally, the individual tests are 'hands on' dexterity tests whereas the group tests tend to be

paper and pencil. There are aptitude tests to measure single aptitudes, e.g. Mechanical reasoning, Computer Programming, Modern Languages and Music. The most common aptitude test experienced by students in schools are Aptitude Test batteries which assess a wide range of aptitudes known as the Differential Aptitude Tests, including Verbal Reasoning, Numerical Reasoning, Abstract

Reasoning, Space Relations, Mechanical Reasoning, Clerical Speed and Accuracy, Spelling and Language use. Aptitude tests enable Guidance Counsellors to predict a student's likely level of performance in specific areas. For example a student who scores highly in a Space Relations aptitude test is showing potential in the field of Architecture or Design.

Guidance counsellors administer such instruments prior to a student making subject choices for the Leaving Certificate. This may take place towards the end of Third year, but as most students now proceed to Transition year, it is more likely to take place towards the end of that year. Alongside a student's performance in school and state examinations, Differential Aptitude Tests can be very useful, in assisting students in clarifying their subject choices for Leaving Certificate.

Achievement Tests
Achievement tests are used in evaluating a student's level of knowledge, skills and competencies. Unlike other kinds of tests, most achievement tests are set by a student's own teachers. Standardised National Achievement tests include the Junior and Leaving Certificate.

Occupational Interest Inventories

These instruments are widely used by Guidance Counsellors to measure a student's occupational interests. Unlike other forms of psychometric instruments used in Guidance Counselling, these inventories are not timed and a student's answers are simply a guideline to his or her thinking on career choice at a particular moment in time. Over time such instruments taken collectively can assist a student to more serious career investigation in a particular area.

Personality Instruments

Personality Instruments are designed to measure what a person is like rather than a person's potential. They are much more complex to both administer and interpret and special training over and above the basic training of a Guidance Counsellor is required to administer and interpret them. Having said that, it is also important to state that measuring the personality of children under sixteen is judged by most professionals as unwise, as a child's personality is very much in formation up to that age. However there is good evidence to suggest that the administration of Personality Instruments, to students between the ages of sixteen to nineteen can be a useful tool, alongside a wide range of other sources of information, in assisting effective career choice.

THE TRANSITION YEAR PROGRAMME

By Brian Mooney,

President of the Institute of Guidance Counsellors

The Transition Year Programme

The Transition year programme was initiated in 1974, but only really took off in most schools in the 1990s. It is designed to promote a range of competencies and skills not usually emphasised within traditional academic education. It places an emphasis on developing personal and social skills, self-directed learning and providing young people with experience of adult and working life. It is very different from the rest of secondary education, in that it provides a broader educational experience and moves students away from the pressure and focus of a terminal exam, for a full year.

About a quarter of the schools offering the Transition Year (TY) programme do so on a compulsory basis. The rest offer it as an option and it is up each student to choose to do it or go straight to fifth year and the Leaving Cert. programme. Currently, twenty five thousand students take the programme annually. Girl's secondary schools are more likely to take Transition Year, with vocational schools least likely to do so. Because of the logistical constraints of providing the programme, smaller schools are less likely to provide it than larger schools. Similarly, schools who are deemed to be more 'disadvantaged' in their student intake are less likely to provide the programme than other schools.

What is the structure of Transition Year?

There are no standardised syllabi, so each each school has the freedom to design its own Transition Year programme. It will comprise a mix of the following:

- Project assignments
- Work experience
- Academic work
- Cultural studies
- Sports/leisure activities
- Computer studies
- Civic/social awareness programmes
- Business activity
- Practical skills
- Third level 'tasters'

Transition Year

Project work features very strongly in many Transition Year programmes; even in adult life, projects tend to get left to the last minute and the experience of completing a project to a deadline is enormously beneficial to students, as it introduces the notion of time management into their academic lives.

A core feature of Transition Year, in almost all cases, is that it provides students with the opportunity to take part in **work experience**. In general students spend an average of fifteen days on work experience, with all schools offering a minimum of one week. Some students use work experience to try out a career they may be interested in. However in other cases, work experience may resemble part-time jobs with students obtaining work experience from their usual part-time job or even choosing placements in which they are likely to be 'kept on' as part time workers.

All schools provide traditional **academic subjects** as part of Transition Year, such as Maths, Irish, English, and a Continental Language. Schools will also provide students with modules of the subjects that they might wish to take in the Leaving Certificate programme. In these programmes, students get to take a module of Biology, Physics, Chemistry, Accounting, Economics, Business, Home Economics Social and Scientific. In this way, they can get a flavour for a subject that they might be considering for the Leaving and are in a better position to evaluate it. Academic subjects represent an important core of the Transition Year programme.

The vast majority of schools provide **cultural studies** (such as Art and Drama), **sports/leisure activities** and **computer studies**. Over three quarters of schools include **civic/social awareness programmes** such as community care programmes, where students visit hospital patients or maybe homes for the elderly where they will help with daily activities. They might visit facilities for mildly mentally handicapped children, where they will get involved in helpful activities.

Many schools engage in enterprise or **business-related activities** such as organising mini companies (where real products or services are delivered for financial return!). They might also organise a visit to local businesses to see how businesses actually operate. Sometimes, students are set the task by their TY business teacher of organising all aspects of a visit to the school by a local businessperson. This is hugely developmental, because students have to sit down and plan every detail of the visit, from who writes the letter of invitation to who organises to book a room, from who thanks them afterwards to who organises a cup of tea!

From a career aspect, the fact that TY students engage in work experience increases their linkages with the labour market. This has a very positive effect, in that it gives them an insight into the nature of the world of work, which they will have to engage with, in a few short years. This can help focus student's minds in the two year Leaving Certificate programme that follows.

Part-time work

It's worth addressing the area of part time jobs. A considerable proportion of students engage in paid part-time employment during Transition Year. Studies show that many students are reluctant to forgo this income in fifth and sixth year, for obvious reasons. IBEC, recognising the disruptive aspect of part-time work for students (and having too much money in an exam year), issued a policy statement to employers in July 2004, calling on all employers not to employ students between September and June in their Junior and Leaving Certificate year.

Two thirds of schools provide **practical skills**. These may involve a full day film studies programme in which the students produce a short film or an Archaeology field trip to a local site of interest.

For **third level taster courses**, one of the most interesting programmes I have observed is the Law module, in which practising Barristers give a course on the legal system and organise a mock trial in the classroom. They will use real cases and the correct procedures. There are national finals from among the most successful teams of students, held in the Four Courts on a number of Saturdays each year in May, where students have to both defend and prosecute cases. I have observed Transition Year students calmly walking into the Supreme Court in wig and gown to argue their case in front of three judges of the Supreme Court! I have also heard judges, possibly in jest, favourably contrasting the courtroom skills of Transition Year students with those of practising barristers who appear before them daily. Many a budding law student has been enthused and encouraged by such experiences.

It's an important time for personal development

As can be seen from the above, the myth that Transition Year is a doss year is just that - a myth. As someone involved in working with Transition Year students for ten years, it is very successful in promoting the personal development of students, as well as their social skills.

It often amazed me, when introducing a group of fifteen year-old boys to a group of elderly residents of an old folks home, how the awkward silence and foot shifting of day one is replaced by animated conversations and real friendships in a matter of months. It often extends to individuals or groups of students organising Christmas or birthday gifts, as well as making visits on weekends outside school time.

Transition Year helps students to mature. Many parents complain about how disorganised it appears in comparison to all other years. My experience is that students who take this programme have a level of maturity when the stresses and strains of the Leaving Certificate descend on them that students who bypass this year often lack.

What the students themselves think

Students questioned about this programme as part of the ESRI research emphasised a number of positive aspects of the programme:

- The opportunity to try out different subjects
- The assistance they received from the Guidance programme with career planning
- The opportunity to acquire different approaches to learning
- The opportunity to take a break from examination pressure
- They felt that they matured and felt more integrated into the school.

It may not be for everyone!

However, students in schools from lower ability classes, where the programme was compulsory, had a more negative perception of the programme. For those students, the compulsory 'extra' year in school appears to increase their disaffection with school, resulting in early school-leaving among some, or underperformance among those who remain on to complete their Leaving Certificate.

TY students <u>do</u> perform better in the Leaving Cert.

A key and determining factor for many parents and students in deciding whether to take Transition Year or not, is whether it improves examination performance in the Leaving Certificate? The answer is a clear YES. A number of studies have been undertaken, comparing the Leaving Certificate results of students who took Transition Year and other who did not. Even when statistical allowance is made for the fact that the more academically gifted and motivated students tend to take Transition Year, the result of the research shows that students who take the programme get higher points scores in their Leaving Certificate.

It is likely that the difference in examination performance relates to a number of diverse factors:

- Firstly, it may relate to greater exposure to the Leaving Certificate examination subjects as a result of spending an extra year in school. Schools are explicitly discouraged from covering a substantial proportion of the Leaving Certificate curriculum with Transition Year students, but the foundation built up within certain subjects will nevertheless contribute to performance in these subjects, at least indirectly

- Secondly, the performance gain may reflect greater maturity on the part of students
- Thirdly, TY participation may help students to select Leaving Certificate subjects which better reflect their interests and abilities and thus contribute to higher performance
- Finally, students may develop a more self-directed approach to learning and study more effectively for their Leaving Certificate.

My advice to parents of children taking the Junior Certificate and considering whether to take Transition Year, is to attend the information evening all schools organise on this subject each year. The success or failure of any programme depends ultimately on the resources put into the programme by the school in question. The most important resource is the Transition Year Coordinator, who is responsible for organising all aspects of the programme in the school. The next most important factor is the staff that the Principal allocates to teach in the programme.

Parents should evaluate all aspects of the programme presented to them and ask all the hard questions. Most schools are very proud of how this programme has grown and matured over the years and are only too happy to have present and past students of the programme speak about their experience of it. One factor, which some parents have to consider, is cost. Because of the wide range of extra curricular activities involved in the programme, the cost can be much higher than any other year in school. It would not be unusual if the programme included a stay in an activity centre for a number of days. This might push up the overall cost to five or six hundred euro per student. However, given that many Transition Year students have paid part-time jobs, some of these costs can be paid out of these funds.

HOMEWORK
&
STUDYING

RORY MULVEY BA, HDip. Ed.

STUDENT ENRICHMENT SERVICES LTD.

Homework & Studying

Of all of the issues facing parents of children in secondary school, homework and study are probably the areas of biggest concern. This section deals with this whole topic in detail. I became especially interested in how students study many years ago; in my role as a Form Master for Fifth Years, I often addressed the parents of my students on the importance of studying. At one meeting it was pointed out that I was always telling their children to study, but never how to do it! As a result of their comments, I interviewed some of my students, asking them to outline exactly how they went about learning a topic, and I was struck by the variety of answers and the overall lack of any plan or structure.

It was the start of fifteen years of research and experiment and I have been teaching students how to maximise the effectiveness of their study time for many years now. We run 'Study Skills seminars' in over 300 hundred schools in Ireland on an annual basis and I will outline the main elements of these for you here. Be aware that I am not suggesting that there is one 'correct' way of studying. Some students find it easier to absorb information visually, others really take to mind mapping, some need to recite out loud and so on. Hopefully, you will come across some ideas that will assist your son or daughter along their road to a successful study format that suits them.

Homework vs Study

Before going any further, it's worth pointing out the distinction between homework and study. Homework refers to exercises given by the teachers for completion by the students at home, which are then submitted for correction. Study refers to all other work done by the student (revision, practising past exam questions etc.) It's an important distinction and if a student can understand the difference between them early in secondary school, he or she will benefit greatly. The point is that it is not enough to be simply keeping up with homework – there must be a constant 'study' activity also.

For parents whose children are going into first or second year there is a great opportunity to help them to develop a good study structure and method. For parents with older students, you may wish to let them read this section themselves...our involvement in their lives tends to be seen as irrelevant or intrusive at the best of times!

Create the right environment

If at all possible, provide your child with a good study environment, away from distractions. They should feel that study is an important part of their day's activities. From an early age try to insist that a certain time is set aside for schoolwork. Ideally, they should have their own work station, folders, pens etc. An atmosphere of study in the home and a genuine respect for school and education will greatly enhance the prospect of success for your child. If you, as the parent, show little respect for school rules (correct uniform, signing student journals, etc.), you cannot expect the child to behave differently. It is important, in front of your children, to back up their teachers and their school and to try to instil a sense of pride in their school.

Boys and girls!

There can be a real difference between the study habits of boys and girls. I realise I am making generalisations but they are worth making on the basis that as a parent, it is always important to be forewarned! Generally speaking, boys are much more 'laid back' - girls seem to take their study more seriously. They have more pride in the presentation of their work and love to experience success. They will worry about being punished or reprimanded by a teacher and will be upset because they "got a docket." For many boys, getting as many dockets as possible is a definite challenge! The whole area of discipline has got to be so different. A lot of boys seem to feel that success at the books comes a poor third to success at sport and success with the girls.

This attitude can cause boys to underachieve in our exam system. Girls, with their more mature attitude to school work, tend to score considerably higher in the Leaving Cert. Boys tend to improve considerably by the time they reach third level, in terms of attitude and their ability to concentrate and apply themselves.

Our role as parents

No one can dispute that the greatest single influence on a child's success in school is the interest shown by the parent. You cannot go wrong by showing a keen interest in what is going on at school. I realise that there is a fine line between interest shown and confrontation / interference - only the individual parent knows where this line exists in their relationship with their child. Hopefully this book will help you to understand what is going on a little better and you can make a positive contribution. Every child needs to have his or her parents show a genuine interest in their progress.

It is a major challenge to help your child navigate their way through the education system. Sometimes there seems to be so many pitfalls and problems facing them that we can begin to despair! However, you can be confident that they'll get there in the end. With plenty of encouragement and interest shown by you, they will succeed. Remember, you are far more influential as parents than you realise.

Motivation

There is no doubt that success in itself is a major motivating force. Once we experience success at something we tend to put more effort into it, and further success follows. We all perform better if we are shown that our effort has been appreciated. I think that sometimes as parents we can be too quick to point out our child's faults. Almost everyone responds well to praise and badly to criticism – we try harder and improve our output in an environment that appreciates our efforts. Thus, the more appreciation that we show our children for efforts made, the greater the return. Underachieving students are often those suffering from low self-esteem. Successful people feel successful…they feel confident. Anything you can do to increase children's confidence in their own ability will be greatly rewarded.

"To instill self belief into someone is to change their life!"

It is important to remember that very good students need praise and encouragement as well. Sometimes we tend to forget the good student, as we concentrate all our efforts on helping to improve the weaker student's confidence.

Classroom 'Work'

Students spend much more time in the classroom than studying at home and yet many students learn very little in class, leaving all the work to be done at home. If they learnt properly in class they would free up a lot of time at home to do other things. They have to be in the class anyway, so why not learn there?

What they must realise is that it's not just the teacher's job to teach - it's the student's job to learn too. Hopefully, the teachers do their job...students must do theirs. Are they actively involving themselves in the learning process?

We try to point out to students a few simple things, like the position they sit in the classroom. If they moved nearer the front would their marks improve? Are they near the 'messers' in the class? Most students are very passive in class - they do nothing, they just sit there. There is no such thing as passive learning - you must be active to learn.

It is important that they learn to get involved in class, otherwise a lot of valuable learning time is lost. It is also important that the teacher has a good impression of your child. It takes very little effort for a student to show the teacher they are interested and the resultant rewards are great! The teacher will go out of his or her way to help an interested student.

The Exam System

We know that the Irish exam system is extremely competitive. Each year, more than 55,000 students sit the Leaving Cert. (and slightly more than this sit the Junior Cert.). Those who finish at the top of the list can go on to study anything they want, the next group can take up almost any course they are interested in, and each time you go down the list more and more doors of opportunity are closing. The system operates a cut-off line every five marks (see Points System chart on *page 51*). With so many students involved, there are hundreds who finish within one or two marks of a cut-off point. The purpose of this section is really to try to ensure that you and your child are doing everything you can to achieve as high a mark as possible in each subject. The wrong side of a cut-off line can change a lot for a student. All we're hoping for is that each student performs to the best of his or her ability – the tips and guidelines that follow will hopefully help!

Goal Setting

It is never too early to introduce your child to the concept of setting goals. Most students can understand this concept clearly when it comes to sports. A swimmer or an athlete will set targets for themselves and then push against that target. If they don't make it, they change the training programme, consult the coach...they do something, and then strive once more. School is perhaps the most competitive environment that students will ever be involved in and yet, most of them have no goals or targets set for themselves. It's important however to keep things in perspective. I'm not suggesting that we do anything to add to the pressure already being experienced by young people...on the contrary, they will feel more in control and more relaxed if they follow some of the guidelines here.

A practical plan for goal setting

Once students get an idea of their future career path for third level, they can estimate how many points they will need. Those students who might not wish to get to third level are slightly harder to motivate but they must be encouraged to get the best Leaving Cert possible and they should equally set themselves a target.

It may not need to be too specific at a young age...getting the points required for a number of third level options might be a sufficient goal. By using the Points Chart, they can then set targets for themselves in each subject. They can see how this will help them to achieve their final goal. Each time they get a school report, they mark in their result beside the goal they had set themselves and they can see if they are on course for their long-term goal. If they see that they are falling behind, they can do something - take some time from one subject and give it to another, get some notes, consult their teacher...at least they do something. Then they strive for the next target. A student measuring their progress like this is much more likely to achieve their goal than the one who just says "I'll try my best and see what happens".

The Points System

Percentage	Grade	Higher	Ordinary
90 - 100%	A1	100	60
85 - 89%	A2	90	50
80 - 84%	B1	85	45
75 - 79%	B2	80	40
70 - 74%	B3	75	35
65 - 69%	C1	70	30
60 - 64%	C2	65	25
55 - 59%	C3	60	20
50 - 54%	D1	55	15
45 - 49%	D2	50	10
40 - 44%	D3	45	5
25 - 39%	E	0	0
10 - 24%	F	0	0
0 - 9 %	NG	0	0

Remember, only the best SIX SUBJECTS count.
The highest possible total is therefore 600 points.

Settings goals and identifying problem areas helps students to think ahead. If you feel it may help, you could introduce a small reward system. Remember to keep rewards small - just tokens of appreciation for effort shown. It is vitally important to emphasise that they will not always achieve their targets - nobody does. They must learn from these disappointments, and try again. Undue pressure by you is of no help...your role is to help, encourage, facilitate and generally keep morale up (keep your own disappointments to yourself please!!)

Short term goals

Try to introduce the concept of short-term goal-setting at a young age. You might encourage them to buy a little notebook to jot down their 'weekly goals'…small things can be achieved each week. If a child states that their goal is 'improve at French', explain that that this is a good thing but it's not quite an achievable goal - it has to be something measurable, something specific. 'I'm going to learn three French words a night' - now that's a goal; you can see if you achieve it. Three French words a night could really make a difference by the time the Leaving Cert. comes around (get them to work out how many words they would learn by the Leaving Cert. if they kept that up!).

Sample page of Goals Notebook.

Goals for week ending: SUNDAY _____

Hist: Finish draft copy of assignment

Maths: Do two questions from past papers each night;
          learn Quadratic Equations

Eng: Read to page 92 in novel
          Get notes on MacDuff from John

Geog: Brief notes on Chap 5 "Rivers"

German: Two new words into Vocab notebook each night and learn

Move places in Maths class
Ask 3 questions each day
Take down 5 new things in each lesson
Give up "Corrie"!

The idea is that each week, they would jot down the five most important things they could do - in order - the most important thing to be achieved is at the top of the list. Each night, they check the list and this helps them to use their time doing the most important things. This concept of prioritising is the central concept of good time management. Many students set themselves very general goals – 'I'll do some extra work in Maths this week'. That's a difficult one to measure and achieve… change this type of goal into something much more specific like 'I will revise ratios and I'll do it for twenty minutes on Thursday at 7.10p.m'.

The more specific the goal, the more the likelihood of it being achieved

How much time…?

A very common question asked by parents and students alike, is how many hours they should be studying at their particular year / level in school. The real issue is that it is not the time they spend, but what they learn that is important.

The amount of time a student can concentrate for is a subject of much debate. A lot of factors come into play, the subject they are studying, how tired they feel, things on their mind, what they did the night before and so on. Our own research shows that most study sessions should only last for 25-30 minutes, followed by a short break and then back for another 25-30 minutes. The initial reaction of most students (and all parents!) is that this is much too short! However, the short sharp session, followed by a little break and then a move to a different subject seems to be the best way to learn and commit knowledge and skills into one's long-term memory.

I'd love to see students go up to their room and give themselves little tasks to complete within short time limits, *"I'm going to solve this Maths problem and I'll have it done in 6 minutes"*. When six minutes is up and they haven't solved the problem, stop anyway! *"Now I'm going to do four pages of Geography, and I'll be finished by 7.25p.m. - go!"* If the students worked like that each night, there would be a lot less day-dreaming.

Good students often hate taking the little regular breaks - they feel that they want to get a lot done at once. They are afraid that the breaks will destroy their night's work. I try to explain the importance of taking breaks with the following story:

Two knights in the kingdom were driving the king mad - each one striving to outdo the other, in trying to prove that he is the fittest, strongest knight in the kingdom. One day, the king decided to end this rivalry once and for all. Each knight was given a big axe and brought out to the forest. The king put each knight at either end of the forest. The first one to cut a path through to the middle by chopping down the trees would be deemed to be the fittest. Well, the signal was given and 'Knight A' was off! He was going to show everyone! He started chopping at a great speed. He could hear, away in the distance, the sound of his rival chopping away. After a short time, he noticed a silence - his opponent was taking a break! This spurred him on to greater things. He decided he would have no breaks - he would work right through, and show everyone! Each time he heard the other knight taking a break, he was delighted and worked even harder. When he got to the centre of the forest, there was the opponent and the king sitting down having their sandwiches!! He couldn't believe it.

"How did you that?" he asked. "I heard you having lots of breaks , and I never had one!"

"That's just the reason," explained the other knight. "Every time I took a break, I was sharpening my axe!"

There are dangers however with the concept of taking a five minute break every thirty minutes or so. The student that goes downstairs for a very short break can still be there twenty minutes later! It is so easy to become distracted and start looking at the telly or making a phone call to a friend. The frequent break idea will only work if they have a specific routine to go through (like reading a quick article in a magazine, chipping ten (and only 10!) golf balls in the back garden or making a cup of coffee / glass of water in the kitchen). They should avoid checking their email or phone messages, definitely avoid getting caught up in a TV programme (even for a quick five minute 'fix') and should plan a specific time to take a bigger break for this type of activity.

A timetable

A timetable is the best way they can make efficient use of their limited time. An organised student will succeed. They may indeed end up having more free time through effective use of a timetable!

The timetable below is for illustrative purposes only. Each student has unique commitments and ambitions and each one must try to construct something realistic that they have a good chance of being able to stick to. They shouldn't be too ambitious at the beginning either - it is better to start with something simple and build it up. In setting up their timetable, they firstly take out time for sports, T.V. shows, jobs, music lessons, etc. - all their committed time. They then divide the time remaining into 25-minute blocks, with 5-minute breaks. This could be adapted to 20 minutes, with 10-minute breaks for younger or weaker students, until they get used to the idea of planning out their study time.

Having constructed a grid of available time, the student now allocates time for their homework. We recommend that they leave their easiest homework to the end of the night, when they are feeling tired. Most students do their easiest homework first, when they are at their freshest! The student should also put aside about 10 or 15 minutes for REVIEW (the purpose of this short session each night will be explained later). They can now allocate some sessions to revise their various subjects.

Homework & Studying

Sample weekly timetable.

MON.	TUES.	WED.	THURS.	FRI.	SAT.	SUN.
5.00-5.25 HOMEWORK			5.00-5.25 ACC.	4.45-5.10 IRISH	9.05-9.30 HOMEWORK	
5.30-5.55 ACC.		DINNER	5.30-5.55 HOMEWORK	5.15-5.30 REVIEW		
DINNER T.V.	DINNER T.V.	6.30-6.55 MATHS	DINNER T.V.	5.35-6.00 PHYSICS		
7.00-7.25 FRENCH	7.00-7.25 HOMEWORK	7.00-7.25 HOMEWORK	7.00-7.25 IRISH	DINNER T.V.	1.15-1.40 PHYSICS	1.00-1.25 MATHS
7.30-7.50 REVIEW	7.30-7.45 REVIEW	7.30-7.45 REVIEW		7.00-7.25 FRENCH		1.30-1.55 IRISH
7.55-8.20 HOMEWORK	7.50-8.15 MATHS			7.30-7.55 "CATCH-UP"*	6.00-6.25 HOMEWORK	
PLAY COMPUTER	8.20-8.45 HOMEWORK		8.30-8.45 REVIEW		6.30-6.55 "CATCH-UP"	6.00-6.20 W/end REVIEW
8.45-9.10 IRISH	PHONE CALLS!		8.55-9.15 ENGLISH			
9.15-9.40 EASIEST H.W.	9.05-9.30 ENGLISH	9.10-9.35 PHYSICS	9.20-9.45 HOMEWORK			9.00-9.25 "CATCH-UP"
	9.35-10.00 EASIEST H.W.	9.40-10.00 EASIEST H.W.				

* "Catch-up" is a time where they can catch up on work not completed on a previous day.

Every week they need a different timetable, because no two weeks are the same. Each Sunday they should plan out the week ahead - set their goals into their "weekly goals notebook" and adjust their basic timetable for the week ahead - there may be a match on the Wednesday, or they may have a French test on the Thursday, and these things have to be taken into account.

For students who find the whole concept of a set weekly timetable completely unrealistic, they could organise a daily timetable - not as good, but better than no timetable at all. There is a danger of spending too much time preparing their timetables, so keep an eye on that too.

Study Timetables are not easy for students to stick to; however, the very act of constructing one is helping the student to think ahead and to plan things out. If a child can learn the basic concepts of good time management at an early age, it will stand to them for the rest of their lives. They will need your encouragement and praise when they begin to use one and will need to feel that it's their project – our role is to provide the support network and to reassure them when frustrations set in…and they will!

"One always has enough time, if only one applies it well"
J.W.Goethe, 1813.

Homework

A lot of students believe that homework is a waste of their valuable time. Older students in particular feel they should get less homework so that they have more time to study what they feel is important. And for an awful lot of students, I would have to agree that they are right - it is almost a waste of their time! The reason I say this is because most students just copy their homework out of their textbook. They have the book open on the table and they just copy the answer out, onto a piece of paper! Some students even call their exercise book a 'copy book' because they use them to copy out the book!!

They need to realise that we learn by making mistakes and then by correcting them (or having them corrected by a teacher). They must lose the fear of being wrong! To answer a task that has been set for them (homework, or practising answers from past exam papers for example), we recommend that they read their textbook first, then close it and attempt to answer the questions. For example, for a geography question, the student looks at the required map in his or her book and then closes it. They then attempt to draw the particular map or diagram (without fear of being wrong). This should be done quickly without too much care for neatness. Next, they should quickly check the book and correct their attempt (they must physically correct it, not just look at the mistakes). This method allows them to learn information much more quickly and effectively. If it's for homework, they may have to repeat it neatly for submission.

Another important aspect of homework, for exam classes particularly, is the time taken to complete the task set. A lot of very good students believe that it is great to spend a long time doing perfect work. These are the very students who come out of exams saying, "I couldn't finish the paper" or "I ran out of time". They must learn that our exam system tests the students against the pressure of the clock. If they never practise under time pressure, they can get mental blocks and under-perform in exams. They must know how long they get for a particular task in the test, and then see if they can complete it within that time limit.

I would not stress this exam timing concept too greatly with younger students, however, it is vital to the exam classes (Third and Sixth Years).

Hopefully, you can now see why homework is perhaps the most important part of the night's work, if done properly. Homework allows one to make mistakes (and have the teacher there next day to correct it); homework teaches exam techniques (working within time limits) and homework tells one what to study ('if I can't do a certain homework, or I do it very badly, then I make a note to myself to study that topic').

The Road to Success – The Three Essentials!

If a student is to succeed in such a competitive environment, he or she needs to possess the "Three Essentials For Success", and this is where we begin all our student seminars. Whether it's sport, business, or anything where there is competition, you must have these three attributes or you will not succeed:

a) Ambition   b) Confidence   c) A Plan

(a) Ambition

Your child will study harder and more effectively if they can set their sights on what they're aiming for. A student who wants to go on to third level has the advantage of knowing the points he or she must achieve to fulfil their ambition. Those who don't think they want to go through third level education need to set themselves a target that they wish to achieve in the Leaving Cert for their own satisfaction. Once a goal is set, a plan can be made as to how to get there. Without the goal or ambition, it becomes a lot harder to motivate and be motivated.

Many students just drift from one week to the next. It is vitally important that they become focused; otherwise time will just disappear on them. Anything you can do to encourage them to aim high, to become ambitious, will help to focus the mind. Perhaps you could bring them to a university or college and encourage them to have a look around; maybe get them to talk to one of your friends who is in a particular career; spend some time in helping them to pick their work experience for school and so on. It is really amazing how much more focused a child is when they feel that there is a real purpose in doing well in the exam. They are never too young to be encouraged to be ambitious.

Very few people work hard at anything if there is no great reward. The greater the perceived reward, the more effort is put in.

(b) Confidence

The second requirement for success is that the student has confidence in his or her own ability. As stated earlier, one of the most important roles we as parents have is to convince our child that they are very good at school - that there is really nothing that will be placed before them that

Homework & Studying

they are not able, with help, to cope with. If they experience success at anything, praise them. Make a big fuss of it. This is important at as early an age as possible. A simple rule of thumb –

if they do well it is due to their ability; if they do badly it is due to a lack of effort.

As parents, one of our principal roles is to try to build up the self worth of our children. Inside every poor, or average student, there is a brilliant achiever yearning to get out! In the early stages, help them to set tasks and targets that are quite easily achievable and then praise them when an achievement is made.

(c) A Plan

The third ingredient on the road to success is a plan. You have all heard the saying that "nobody plans to fail, all they do is they fail to plan". No student wants to do poorly, but very few of them have any plan as to how they are going to achieve their potential.

It's not enough just to hope, or even to believe you can do something - you must plan out how you are going to achieve it. The main difference between successful people and the rest of humanity is that successful people set goals (measurable targets) and write them down.

"Remember, you are always a success once you try."

The Art of Note-taking

Many students waste a lot of their time writing summaries rather than taking notes. Some students find this a time consuming exercise and end up not taking notes at all! You could help them to save hours of their valuable time by teaching them the basic fundamentals of taking notes. Try the following exercise with your child.

Using the sample passage below, ask your child to take notes. Time them, and when they finish, ask them to count up the number of words they used (most tend to halve the length of the original passage). Show them what they could have done by referring to the example given. As they get good at note taking, they will be able to reduce their work a lot more than in our example (they will begin to use their own shorthand and to leave out the things that they knew already).

They should be able to cut their notes down into very short checklists of information. These short lists are what they use when studying.

Sample Passage:

Tropical Cyclones are called by a variety of names. In the USA, Mexico and the Caribbean they are called hurricanes. In the western North Pacific and China Sea they are called typhoons. In the Australian, Indonesian and African regions they are generally referred to as cyclones.

The centre of the tropical cyclone is called the eye, the area of lowest pressure. The eye is calm and often has no cloud cover. The width of the eye can vary from a few kilometers to more than 150 kilometers in diameter, but the average is about 30 kilometers.

Around the eye is a wall of cumulonimbus clouds where winds may exceed 300 kilometers per hour, accompanied by torrential rains. This zone extends to 80 kilometers from the eye and causes destruction on a vast scale. Gale force winds may be experienced up to 100 kilometers in the path of a cyclone but they do not extend far behind the main speed-ring after a cyclone has passed.

Sample Notes:

CYCLONES

1. NAMES:

       a) Hurricane - US, Mex, Carib.

       b) Typhoon - NW Pac., China Sea

       c) Cyclone - S. Pac., India, Africa

2. EYE:

       a) Lowest pressure

       b) Calm, no cloud

       c) Diameter - few to 150km (avg. 30km)

3. AROUND EYE:

       a) Cumulonimbus cloud

       b) Wind > 300kph i) vast destruct.

                 ii) Torrential rain

       c) Extends to 80k

       d) Gales in front; little wind behind.

There are, of course, many different ways of taking notes, some much more creative than the outline method shown above. The main thing is for the student to reduce their work into short, manageable notes which are quick to construct and easy to learn.

They need to use this note-taking method for all their study and reviewing activity. Let's take a closer look at that now.

The Art of Studying and Reviewing:

It is not the time students spend studying, but the method that they use, that is important. We base everything we teach our students on "The Principle of Learning" - i.e. that you learn by making mistakes.

What I am outlining below is a quick version of our 'S.E.S. Method of Learning'. It will not be possible here to go into a great amount of detail, but this quick method should show instant results and will suit children of all ages.

Before the student begins studying a topic, they should quickly test themselves. They jot down roughly on a piece of paper everything they can remember about the topic - no matter how little. If they are not sure, they guess - they must never be afraid to be wrong! They must try really hard - spending a full three minutes doing this.

They then open the book and quickly read through the relevant section.

The next thing to do is to take brief notes. If they come across an important diagram, they close the book and practise it, open the book and correct their attempt. When they have worked like this for about twenty minutes, they stop and close all notes and books.

Now comes the important part! They must quickly test their knowledge by jotting down all they *now* know. This can be done in two minutes - they don't write sentences, just key words. Once again they check their notes to see how they did – was every main element recalled and so on.

Anytime in the future that they wish to study this topic again, they just 'Review' it. To 'Review', they quickly jot down all they know without looking at any notes or books (in three minutes). They then compare this to their good notes to see how they went. Each night in their timetable, they set aside some time for Reviewing. It's this continual Reviewing that locks in the factual information. It's so quick that most students don't mind doing a little each night. On its own, this method is not sufficient. However, by doing their homework properly, it allows them to practise putting the information into the format they will require for their exams. Each night the student learns a few new things, reviews information previously learnt and then practises the exam by doing homework! If they work from a method like this, they begin to see real progress being made and this increases their confidence in their own ability.

Once they achieve a bit of success, they begin to feel successful. The old saying "success breeds success" really begins to kick in.

The exams & all that pressure:

Unfortunately, study on its own does not guarantee success. Two students with the same knowledge can finish up with vastly different results in the exam. It always amazes me how poor some students' exam techniques are. You would be astounded at how many scripts are handed in unfinished! Another major problem is that many students misread the question asked, or simply do not understand what the examiner is looking for.

Exam time can be very stressful for many students and their parents. Households are filled with tension as June approaches. Everybody moves about on tenterhooks so as not to upset the "exam student". For some unfortunate students the fear of doing badly can ruin the last few weeks of study time.

As the exams approach, do your best to encourage your child to get a good night's sleep. They should not be cramming late at night. They need their rest (ideally eight hours a night), a good diet and some exercise. Moderate exercise is a wonderful way for them to relieve stress. Try to discourage them from taking stimulants - excessive coffee, or pills that help you stay awake. These can harm their ability to think clearly and logically. Recent research in the U.K. has shown that students should be hydrated when they are studying. The difference in concentration levels between hydrated and dehydrated students varied by up to 30%. The average student should be drinking about two and a half litres of water a day - not soft drinks, tea or coffee - just plain water.

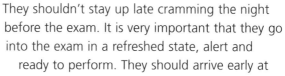

They shouldn't stay up late cramming the night before the exam. It is very important that they go into the exam in a refreshed state, alert and ready to perform. They should arrive early at the exam centre, there is no worse way to prepare than getting agitated in a traffic jam on the way to your exam!

Quite a number of students tend to underachieve because of the pressure they put themselves under. While there is no doubt that a certain level of stress will improve performance levels, too much stress, (distress), will certainly impair performance. Some students get so stressed that they experience mental blocks, end up misreading the question, get the timing of the paper wrong, or just panic! The main cause for this undue stress is a lack of practice. Everyone is scared by the unknown, the unexpected. We can scream aloud, and almost jump out of our seat, at a scary horror movie. We then rent the movie and invite our friends around and scream again. However, having watched it a few times, we know what to expect and we even end up laughing at it. We become immune by knowing what to expect. It is somewhat similar with the Leaving / Junior Cert. If we practise often enough we almost know how we are going to do before we sit the exam. There are no real surprises in store.

Each year the students are told how many questions they will have to answer in each subject, they are told how many marks (and therefore exactly how much time they should spend) for every question. They have access to all the previous years' papers. The marking schemes are also available. There is even an Examiners Report on how the students of a particular year fared in that year's paper. With all this information, nothing should be unexpected!

They are allowed to practise the exam every day, if they want to, and get it corrected by a teacher. However, as we all know, very few avail of all this information or practise the exam at all. They seem to only practise exam techniques in the exam itself! Many exam class students do not even know how long they get to do each individual question!

I am convinced that it is a lack of planning and practice that causes exam pressure and resultant mental blocks. The book of past papers is probably one of the most important books they have for each subject. You should get this for them as early in the year as possible.

A few final thoughts:

Our role is to be positive and supportive. My experience is that most problems resolve themselves and come and go in phases. It's important that you keep your cool and consistency as much as possible, that you don't over-react to changing circumstances. Remember that what you worried about last year will be replaced by a whole new worry this year! Hopefully this article and indeed the whole book will provide you with a greater insight as to what your student child is going through. By knowing a little bit more about their school lives and issues, your support and encouragement will be all the more effective. Try and be positive, patient, firm and understanding. Don't expect praise or thanks but know that it will come in time! Good luck.

Rory Mulvey – www.studentenrichment.ie

JUNIOR CERTIFICATE SUBJECTS

Junior Certificate Irish

The main aim of the Irish junior certificate course is to help students develop their speaking, listening and writing skills in the Irish language. It builds on the basics learned at primary school and helps students develop an awareness of the Irish language and Irish literature.

The course can be broken down as follows:

Language skills

Students build on their grammar skills from primary school. This section involves the correct use of nouns, verbs, cases and tenses, as well as adjectives and pronouns. It is essential that students have a good understanding of language skills for both writing and speaking Irish.

Written language

Higher-level students will practise writing essays, short stories, debates and newspaper articles. They will also learn the skills of writing conversations and interviews. Writing letters is also a part of this section and particular importance is given to the layout and correct openings/endings for formal and informal letters. Students will also develop comprehension skills. These will be taught through the reading of short passages and then answering a series of questions about the content.

The format for ordinary level students is slightly different. Students use pictures to prompt story/essay writing. Students are given a series of pictures on which to base their story.

Comprehension skills are developed through the use of notices and unseen poetry or prose. Students will also learn the correct phrases and layout for postcards and letters.

Prose literature

For higher-level students only.

Teachers will select various short stories, dramas or novels which students will study throughout the three years of the junior cycle. Students should be familiar with the title, the author and a summary of the work. Students should also be able to identify the emotion of the work, the plot or theme as well as the characters and the literary techniques used. In the examination, students will also be given some unseen prose to evaluate and comment upon.

Poetry

Again, only on the higher-level course.

A selection of poetry will be taught throughout the three years and like the prose section, students will have to be able to identify emotions, main thoughts, themes and tones in the poems. Students must also know the title, author and the poetical techniques used. In the examination, students will also get some unseen poetry on which they must answer questions or make comment.

ASSESSMENT

Assessment is through a combination of written and aural (listening and comprehension) examinations. There is no oral at junior cert level. The aural examination takes place at the same time as the written examination and is worth 31% of the overall marks. Students must listen to a passage and answer questions. The written examination will examine students' writing and literature skills, depending on the level taken. Junior certificate Irish is also examined at foundation level

Junior Certificate English

The main aim of the Junior Certificate English course is to continue and build on skills developed at primary level. The course aims to develop literacy skills on a personal, social and cultural level.

The course may be looked at under the following headings:

Reading

Students practice reading a variety of texts from different sources such as newspapers and magazines. They answer questions or write commentaries on them. Higher-level students should also be able to identify the different styles of writing and techniques used in the different texts.

Writing

Students develop their writing skills in this section. Good quality of spelling and a knowledge of the rules of grammar are essential. Students practise writing a variety of compositions such as personal interest stories, imaginative essay and current topics. Higher-level students will be expected to be able to write narrative, discursive and descriptive essays.

Students will also learn the writing skills necessary to compose texts they might use on an everyday basis. Letters (formal and informal), reports, diaries, emails and faxes are composed. Students learn the correct phrases and layouts associated with each type. Students also learn how to write descriptions and reviews of films, books and speeches. All elements call on the student's knowledge of grammar, vocabulary and writing techniques.

Media studies

Students look at and analyse the power of the media in informing and persuading the public. Film, posters, advertising, newspapers and so on are all examined and compared. Students will become familiar with terms such as broadsheets, slogans, captions and tabloids.

Poetry

Students will study a set number of poems depending on the level they are studying at. Students must know the poet, the title of the work and the poet's background. They must also be able to discuss the poem under headings such as theme, language, imagery, rhythm and style. Students must be able to form an opinion about the poem, giving valid reasons why they like or dislike it. They must also be able to compare and contrast different poems.

Fiction

Students will read a novel as chosen by their teacher. They must be able to discuss and comment on its plot, theme, main characters and the development of the story or main ideas. Students should also be aware of the style of writing and the context in which it was written.

Drama

Again, students will study a play/s as selected by their teacher. They must be able to write about the plot, theme, characters and style. They must be able to discuss the main characters, and their relationship with each other. They will also study the background to the drama i.e. costumes, song, dance, props and how they all contribute to setting the atmosphere of the play.

ASSESSMENT

Assessment is in the form of a written paper and is examined at three levels – higher, ordinary and foundation.

Junior Certificate Mathematics

There are eight areas in Higher and Ordinary level and there are seven areas in Foundation level (trigonometry is not included). Junior Cert maths consists of two papers each with six questions. Each question is compulsory and contains three parts. The eight areas are explained below:

Set theory

This is a new concept for the first year student. Set theory tests the student's problem-solving and organisational skills. Pupils are presented with information which they must interpret, manipulate and arrange into Venn Diagrams (interlocking circles). The language used in set theory involves a series of symbols which students must be able to understand and apply. An enjoyable topic for most students once they get to grips with the terminology involved.

Number systems

Up until now, students will only have dealt with natural numbers. They will now be introduced to a whole new range of number systems, from real to rational numbers. Understanding number systems and the various symbols used to represent them is a must for all students as it provides a basis for all other topics on the course. In recent years, the intelligent use of calculators has been introduced in fourth class at primary school. This is continued at second level and is now allowed in the Junior Cert exam. Other key concepts studied are estimation, approximation, fractions and decimals.

Applied Arithmetic and measure

Possibly the most relevant area of the course to everyday life and work, this section covers the calculation of area and volume. Students will need to be able to recall and apply the various formulae for area and volume. Topics such as taxation, 'Pi' (a value of 22/7), percentages, ratios and proportion are also covered.

Algebra

A difficult topic for some students to grasp as it involves abstractions and generalisations. However, it is an extremely important area to master, as it not only pops up in other sections of the maths course but also in other school subjects. Algebra involves mathematical equations using letters and numbers. Students must be able to solve the equation to find the value of the letters. A basic example would be:

If   x + 5 = 18, find the value of x.

Statistics

A section of the course most students find enjoyable and one that they can relate most readily to their everyday life. Sports results, goals scored, exam averages are all calculated using some form of statistics. Students learn how to calculate percentiles and averages and how to represent statistical information in the form of bar charts, pie charts and so on.

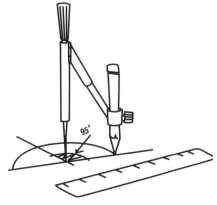

Geometry

While most students will unknowingly have been introduced to geometry in Primary school through the study of space, shape and symmetry, geometry at second level is a whole new ball game. A lengthy topic, it ranges from transformations and co-ordinate geometry (some of us will have used co-ordinate geometry whilst playing battleships at the back of class!) to the dreaded theorems and Pythagoras. The new syllabus has reduced the number of theorems which have to be learned by heart, and concentrates more on the student's ability to understand the proofs and their applications.

Functions and graphs

Students are required to be able to represent mathematical statements in graph form. Accuracy and neatness are essential skills for graph drawing. Having proudly completed either a u-shaped or n-shaped graph, students are then asked a series of questions which they must use their graph to answer.

Trigonometry (higher and ordinary level)

This section involves the study, measurement and construction of angles. New areas of learning include the use of terms such as sine, cosine and tangents. The use of everyday examples like construction and the angle of a football going into a goal make it more concrete and easier to understand for students.

ASSESSMENT

Junior Certificate Maths is examined at three levels: Higher, Ordinary and Foundation.

Junior Certificate Geography

The geography syllabus aims to give students an overall understanding of physical, social and economic geography. Students also learn the practical skills of map reading and how to interpret aerial photographic evidence.

The course is divided into the following sections:

Physical geography

In this section students are introduced to the physical features of the earth such as volcanoes, types of rocks, soil, atmosphere and climate.

Students also investigate the effects of weathering (a study of a limestone region) and erosion by rivers, moving ice and the sea on the earth's physical features.

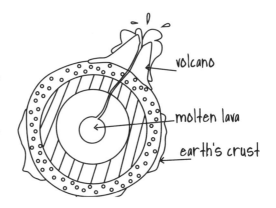

volcano

molten lava

earth's crust

Social geography

Here students investigate the different population cycles in developed and developing countries. The effects of population growth, density and migration are examined. Another topic explored is settlement and urbanisation. Students will look at Irish settlements, nucleated settlements and new settlements. They will investigate the functional use of land, urban problems and the consequences for developing infrastructure.

Economic geography

A slight overlap here with the business studies course in the examination of primary, secondary and tertiary sectors of industry. Natural resources (oil, peat, fishing and farming) are studied and students also examine the economic activities associated with these natural resources through manufacturing systems. Industrial locations are examined through the use of case studies. The role of women in industry in either China or Russia is explored as well as the important issue of economic inequality.

Ordnance survey map reading and aerial photograph interpretation

A practical skill that most students find enjoyable, students are taught how to read maps and how to interpret aerial photographs. They will look at the location and development of towns, urban functions and the different uses of land. They will learn how to identify physical features, settlement patterns, tourist attractions and communication networks.

ASSESSMENT

Junior certificate geography is examined at both ordinary and higher levels. The assessment takes the form of a written examination based on the whole course and requires students to write brief descriptive paragraphs or to use practical skills in the form of map reading. There is also the option of completing a field study, based on research. Those who take this option will be exempt from part of the examination paper.

History

History at Junior Cycle requires students to show that they understand the main trends, issues and events covered in their syllabus. It calls on students' abilities to interpret and analyse information. They must also be able to differentiate between fact and opinion as well as recognising the differences between primary (first hand/eye witness) and secondary (second hand) sources. Students will also learn how to develop lines of argument and are expected to be able to back up all statements with facts and explanations. The key to success in history is being able to assimilate all relevant information without padding out answers with irrelevant information!

The history course has been divided into three main sections as follows:

1. How we find out about the past

Higher level and Ordinary level students must study all sections.

General **introduction** to history, the role of the historian and an exploration of the different types and sources and evidence.

Our roots in ancient civilisation: Students use archaeological based evidence to study the houses, family life, working life and day-to-day customs in pre-Christian and early Christian Ireland. Students will also study one other ancient civilisation.

Castle, church and city: This involves the study of medieval society, cities, castles, monasteries and parishes. Students will use settlements from local, national and international sources to aid their study.

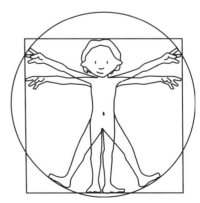

Renaissance: This section of part 1 draws on visual sources and biographies to assist students in studying the art, architecture, printing and learning of the Renaissance era in various countries across Europe.

2. Studies of Change

In this section the course offers both general studies and special studies. Higher-level students are expected to cover all aspects while Ordinary level students may concentrate on the 'special studies'.

Changes in European views of the world:

General Study: this part of the course introduces students to exploration; why people wanted new sea routes, how voyages were possible and the main consequences of these voyages.

Special Study: An account of one exploration

Religious Change:

General Study: An exploration of the Reformation, why it occurred and the main consequences.

Special Study: The Life of one Reformer and the effect he had.

Changes in land ownership:

General Study: A look at how and why land changed hands and the effect it had on politics, culture and religion.

Special Study: One plantation in Ireland

Political Change:

General Study: A study of both the sources of discontent and the revolutionary movements in America, France and Ireland, and the consequences of these revolutions in the late 18th and early 19th centuries.

Special Study: The life of one revolutionary in America, France or Ireland.

Social Change:

General Study: This section looks at the agricultural society in the 18th century. Students will learn about the factors which influenced the agricultural and industrial revolutions and the effects they had on people's lives.

Special Study: Contrasting lifestyles c. 1850: Industrial England and Rural Ireland.

Junior Cert. Subjects

3. Understanding the Modern World

In part 3, Ordinary level students must study International relations in the 20th century and one other topic. Higher-level students are required to study all three of the following topics

Political Developments in Ireland in the late 19th century and in the 20th century:

Students will learn about the main political events that took place which have had a major impact on contemporary Ireland.

Social Change in the 20th century:

In this section students analyse social change in different contexts. They will look at the changing lifestyles in Ireland from c. 1900 either in their local area or at a national level. They will then compare their findings with a contrasting society such as the USA.

International Relations in the 20th century:

Students will study peace and war in Europe from 1920 – 1945. They will look at the sources of conflict and the strategies that were used to restore peace. Students will also look at one of the following from 1945 – present: *The rise and fall of the Superpowers* or *Moves towards European Unity* or *African and Asian nationalism.*

ASSESSMENT

Both higher and ordinary levels are assessed by a written exam. There are a variety of questioning techniques used such as the identification of pictures and documents, short answer questions and general questions, requiring paragraph answers.

Junior Cert Subjects

Junior Certificate French

French is one of the most popular foreign languages offered in Irish schools today. This course is designed to help students to become proficient in speaking, listening to, reading and writing the French language.

The main syllabus sections are as follows:

Grammar:

Students must become familiar with the following tenses of verbs

- Présent
- Passé composé
- Imparfait
- Futur
- Conditionnel (higher level)

The correct use of prepositions such as à, de, en etc.

The use of possessive adjectives such as mon, ton, etc.

The correct formation of questions.

The correct use of pronouns both subject and object (higher level)

Written Expression

Students will learn the following forms of written expression

- Message writing – writing a short note or an informal message
- Postcard writing – learn the standard format and use informal vocabulary about holiday activities, weather, plans etc.
- Letter writing – learn common expressions and vocabulary for informal letters to friends, relatives and pen pals about topics such as hobbies, interests, yourself, etc.

Higher-level students will be required to be able to write formal letters about topics such as making reservations and requesting information.

Reading Comprehensions

Students will learn how to read and interpret a passage in French and to answer questions about the passage through English.

Listening Comprehensions

This section involves students listening to a passage or dialogue in French and being able to answer a series of questions based on the passage.

ASSESSMENT

The French course is assessed by a combination of a written examination and a listening comprehension. The written examination assesses reading comprehension and written expression and is worth 56%. The listening comprehension takes place just before the written examination and is worth 44%. Here, students will listen to spoken passages in French and are required to answer a number of questions through English.

Junior Certificate Civic, Social and Political Education (C.S.P.E.)

The CSPE course was designed to introduce students to all aspects of our civic, political and social structures. It teaches them what it means to be a citizen and helps them to develop skills for citizenship. Students are also introduced to Ireland's political structure, the State and government at local, national and international levels. Finally, students learn what a community is, at school, at home and in their locality.

The course is divided up into 4 main units as follows:

The Individual and Citizenship:

This section of the course concentrates on helping students to build awareness of what it means to be a good citizen. Emphasis is placed on the concepts of Human Dignity and Stewardship. Overall, there is an exploration of citizenship in various contexts such as at home, at school and at local, national and international levels.

The Community:

In this section the concept of Democracy is explored. Students will compare different communities, their characteristics, origins, representations and structures. Students learn that development and change are important aims of most communities.

The State – Ireland:

Leading on from the last section, students learn that the state is made up of many different communities. Students learn how decisions at national level can be influenced by communities and organisations. Students also learn about our electoral system and our legal and judicial systems. The concepts of Democracy, Law and Rights and Responsibilities form the core of this unit.

Ireland and the World:

Students will investigate Ireland's membership of the various international organisations such as the EU and UN. They will learn how Ireland can contribute to important world issues. The key concepts in this unit are Development and Interdependence.

Junior Cert. Subjects

ASSESSMENT

CSPE is assessed by both a written examination (40%) and either an Action Project or Course-work Assessment Book (60%). The Course-work Book requires students to report on two modules from their course. For the assessment of the Action Project, the actual project is not submitted but rather, students are required to write a detailed description/report on their project.

Junior Certificate Business Studies

The business studies syllabus is designed to prepare students for the commercial world. It gives students an insight into managing money on a personal and national level as well as an understanding of the economic environment.

The business studies course can be divided into the following sections:

Business of living:

In this section, students will learn the following topics:

- Budgeting – a look at income, expenditure and household budgeting and accounts.
- Consumer education – here students are made aware of consumer rights and protection.
- Financial services – a look at money and banking, credit, borrowing facilities and insurance.

Economic Awareness and Business Background:

National Business - This section looks at economic resources and how the economy is organised. The National Budget is explored and students learn about the importance of international trade and Ireland's membership of the EU.

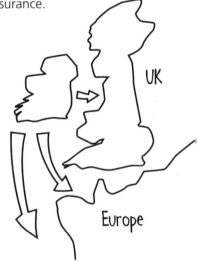

Business Units. Students are introduced to the different types of business organisations such as the sole trader, co-ops, public companies and semi state bodies. Students will explore the relative advantages and disadvantages of each type of organisation. Private limited companies are explored in greater detail, looking at their formation in a variety of legal entities.

Work. Students learn about the chain of production, employment and unemployment and the organisational structure of the workplace. The rights and responsibilities of employers are discussed as well as learning how to employ staff, calculate wages, fill out tax forms and keep employee records. Finally students investigate the relationship between management and employees, trade unions and industrial relations.

Services to Business. In this section, students learn how businesses raise capital, plan their finances and future and the types of insurance they may need. Commercial banking is also explored as are communications.

Enterprise:

This section deals mainly with the following topics:

- Marketing - Students learn the various marketing and communication techniques employed by businesses

- Transport – This involves distribution and delivery systems used by businesses.

- Business transactions and documents – Here students learn the practical side of business, through learning how to write business letters and reports. They also learn how to complete documents such as invoices, quotations and order and delivery notes.

- Bookkeeping - A break from business theory, this section involves students learning the skills of double entry bookkeeping and keeping accounts. Students will learn how to record and complete sales and purchases, cashbooks, general journals etc. This section also involves finding profit and loss, trading accounts, balance sheets, making adjustments to final accounts and how to assess a business. While higher-level students must cover all elements of this section, ordinary level students are required only to cover petty cash books and some aspects of the profit and loss accounts.

Information Technology:

In this final section students learn all about computers, their hardware and software. The advantages and disadvantages of computers are also discussed as well as the use of computers both in the home and in a business.

ASSESSMENT

Business studies are assessed at both higher and ordinary levels. Higher-level students have two written examinations, while ordinary level students complete one written examination.

Junior Certificate Religious Education

Religious Education has just recently been introduced as a subject for national certification. The course encourages students to explore various religions, in particular Christianity, and how they have contributed to the culture in which we live. While students will have to draw on their own experience in the examination, the student's own personal faith and affiliations to certain religions will not be subject to examination.

The course has been broken up into two main parts:

Part 1

Students may select any two of the following sections:

Communities of Faith

Students are required to explore the nature and patterns of human communities of faith, both at national and international levels. The relationships between these communities will also be examined. Higher-level students will examine the organisation and leadership structures in communities of faith.

Foundations of Religion – Christianity

The main objective of this section is to explore the context into which Jesus was born. Students will study evidence about Jesus, the person and the preaching of Jesus as well as the meaning of His death and resurrection for His followers, both in the past and the present day.

Foundations of Religion – Major World Religions

In this section students explore in detail the major religions of the world such as Buddhism, Hinduism, Islam and Judaism. They will look at sources of evidence, rites of passage, development of tradition and other rituals. Higher-level students will also look at tradition, faith and practice in today's world.

Part 2

Students are required to study all of the following sections:

The Question of Faith

Here, students explore religious faith today and will identify and recognise the characteristics and foundations of religious faith. Higher-level students will be required to explore challenges to faith. This section also allows all students to explore and reflect on their own personal faith positions

The Celebration of Faith

This section of the course reflects on how worship and ritual have always been a part of the human response to the mystery of God. The power of signs and symbols as well as prayer will also be discussed. Higher-level students will explore the relationship between patterns of worship and mystery as it applies to individuals and communities.

The Moral Challenge

Here students are introduced to the concept of morality, its sources and how it can be expressed in a variety of ways. They will also explore the moral visions of two major world religions, one of which will be Christianity. Higher-level students will be introduced to some aspects of the relationships between religion, morality and state law.

ASSESSMENT

Religious Education will be assessed at Higher and Ordinary levels. The assessment consists of both a written paper and journal work. The written exam will cover the whole course and questions will take the form of a variety of multiple choice questions, writing of paragraphs, analysis and interpretation of data, photographs and cloze passages.

For their journal, students will have to select a title from a set of twelve titles, which is provided to schools each year. The work may be done individually or as a group.

Junior Certificate Science

This new revised syllabus has been designed to cater for students of all abilities. It is much more activity-based than the previous syllabus and emphasises the practical experience of science. Through investigations and experiments, students develop science processing skills and a knowledge of the underlying concepts.

The course has been broken down into three main sections as follows:

Biology

In this section of the course students will learn about human and plant biology. Students will learn how the human body functions, develops and changes over time. Since plants are a main food source for all living things, their importance is studied through a discussion of both plants and micro organisms.

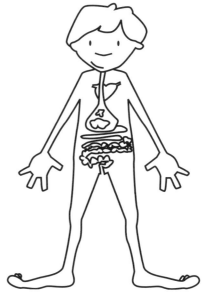

The biology section is further broken down into the following parts:

Human Biology – food, digestion and associated body systems; the skeletal/muscular system, the senses and human reproduction

Animals, plants and micro-organisms.

Chemistry

The study of chemistry provides students with a better understanding of our material world and the processes by which materials change. Students will also learn about how some of these materials and substances occur naturally and how they can be combined to form new materials. Again, this section is divided into the following:

- Classification of substances
- Air, oxygen, carbon dioxide and water
- Atomic structure, reactions and compounds

Physics

This section helps students explore and investigate the laws and relationships that govern our world and how things work The main parts that make up this section are:

- Force and Energy
- Heat, light and sound
- Magnetism, electricity and electronics

ASSESSMENT

The Junior Certificate Science course is examined at both higher and ordinary levels. The assessment involves both a written examination and coursework. There are a set number of compulsory experiments, which are specified in the syllabus. Students will be required to keep a record of all experiments and investigations over the three years which will then be submitted for assessment. This section is weighted 10% of the overall marks. In addition to the compulsory experiments, students are required to carry out two further investigations in third year from a list supplied to the schools each year. Students must submit a report on these investigations to obtain a maximum of 25% of the overall mark. The remaining 65% is awarded for a written examination based on all sections of the course.

LEAVING CERTIFICATE SUBJECTS
(TOP 15)

Leaving Certificate Irish

The Irish course at Leaving Certificate builds on and develops key skills learned at Primary and Junior levels. Students not only improve on their language and written skills but are also introduced to Irish literature and culture.

The course can be described as follows:

Written language

This is a follow on from junior cycle and students enlarge their vocabulary and knowledge of grammar. Students will practice writing essays about topical issues, stories, articles for newspapers, debates, speeches, letters and dialogues. Students will also improve their comprehension skills by reading extracts from papers and magazines and answering questions about the content of the passage.

Prose

Students will study a prescribed selection of texts (novels, stories) or can study a selection of texts from different genres (folktale, drama, short story) of their own (teacher's) choice. Students must study five prose texts. The texts will be studied and discussed under the following headings:

- The main characters
- The theme
- The main ideas

Students should also be able to give an account of the story. Higher-level students must study an additional prose section, where again they have the choice of studying four prescribed texts or their own choice from a collection of short stories, a novel, an autobiography and a drama.

Poetry

There are five prescribed poems on the course, which students may study, or like the prose, they can select five of their own. Higher-level students must study a further eight poems. When studying the poetry students will discuss them under the following headings:

- The main ideas of the poem
- The emotions
- The techniques, images, contrast etc.
- The background of the poem

Students should also be able to express their own feelings about the poems.

History of Irish

This section is for higher level only. Students will study topics such as Irish as a language, different dialects, Irish poets/writers, the decline of Irish and Irish today.

ASSESSMENT

Assessment takes the form of three parts – oral, aural (listening skills) and written examinations. The oral examination takes place a month or so before the final written exam. Students will engage in conversation with the examiner in Irish. The aural exam takes place on the same day as the written paper. Students must listen to a series of dialogues/passages and answer questions about the content. The written exam will examine all elements of the course.

Leaving Cert. Subjects

Leaving Certificate English

The English syllabus centres around two general areas – comprehending and composing. In the comprehending assignments, students will discover how language shapes experience through style and context. In their composing assignments, students will develop skills to use language to shape and order experience for themselves. The syllabus aims to create a respect and recognition for language used accurately and a proficiency in oral and written language skills. The syllabus also aims to give students an appreciation for English literature and poetry.

The course can be broken down into the following sections:

Writing skills

Students will explore different writing styles such as argument, persuasive and narrative. Students will be required to possess a good technique for pre-writing, drafting, editing and proof reading. The composition is the most important question in the written examination (25% of total marks).

Comprehension skills

In this section students have to learn to interpret, evaluate and question texts and identify their style. Through practice, students will be able to comprehend texts at a primary level and also understand the meaning behind these texts.

Literature

This is broken down into a single text and a comparative study. In the single text, students undertake a detailed study of a prescribed text e.g.Wuthering Heights, Macbeth etc. Students will need to have a deep understanding of the text under such headings as theme, character, style, imagery, language and social setting. In recent years the syllabus has allowed some films to be studied. E.g. 'A Room with a View'. In the section, known as a comparative study, students are required to compare and contrast three texts under various criteria. In ordinary level, students are expected to be able to discuss the texts under headings like theme, social setting, and aspects of story. Students at higher level must also know the literary style of the text as well as its cultural context, themes and issues.

Poetry

Students will study a prescribed list of poetry as set by the Dept. of Education. Students will be required to study the poems and comment on their theme, tone, language, imagery, symbols and style. In the examination, students will also be questioned on unseen poetry. The objective of this is for students to identify the theme of the poem and to offer their opinion of it.

ASSESSMENT

English is assessed at both Higher and ordinary levels. Both levels are assessed by a written examination. All elements of the syllabus will be examined.

Leaving Certificate Mathematics

The aim of the Leaving Certificate Mathematics course is to help to provide students with mathematical knowledge, skills and understanding for everyday life. It develops their problem solving and communication skills and their ability to handle abstractions and present logical arguments. It is intended to build on and develop those skills already learned at Junior Cycle level.

The course can be divided up into the following main topics, some of which are common to all levels, (Higher, Ordinary and Foundation) some exclusive to one particular level.

Algebra

For all levels, this builds on the basics of algebra learned at Junior Cycle. It involves the use of variables to stand for unknown numbers. Depending on the level of maths being studied, students will be introduced to solving simple, simultaneous and quadratic equations. All three levels of Maths will have some algebra content.

Arithmetic

This involves the study of maths in terms of practical problems and is common to the ordinary and foundation levels. Students will study ratios, percentages, wages, volume, area, compound interest and so on.

Geometry

This topic is common to all three levels, with the degree of difficulty increasing as the levels increase. Students will study theorems, co-ordinate geometry of the line and circle, transformations; higher-level students will also study vectors.

Trigonometry

Trigonometry involves the study and measure of angles.

Sequences and Series

A topic for ordinary level and higher-level students only, it involves the study of geometric and arithmetic sequences and series, logs and indices. A mastery of algebra will aid students in this section and higher-level students will also be required to study binomial expansions.

Functions, Graphs and Calculus

This topic is studied at both ordinary and higher levels. It involves representing functions by means of a graph. At ordinary level, students will study differentiation, which is the study of rates of change. In addition higher-level students will also study integration, which is connected with the measurement of area and volume.

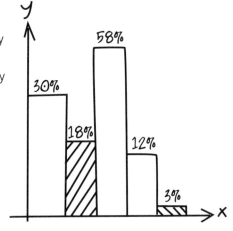

Probability and statistics

The study of statistics involves finding averages, modes, frequencies etc. of data and the representation of information in graph format. This section is studied at all three levels. The probability part involves the study of chance, permutations and combinations. Students at higher level also study difference equations.

Complex Numbers and Matrices

Students at ordinary level will study complex numbers and will learn how to add, multiply and divide these numbers, the rules associated with them and how to solve complex equations. In addition, students at higher level will study matrices, in particular how to add and multiply them. This topic is not studied at foundation level.

Area and Volume

This involves the use of formulae to find the area and volume of different plane objects, such as spheres, cylinders, discs etc. It is studied at both ordinary and foundation levels.

OPTIONAL TOPICS

At both higher and ordinary levels, students are also required to study one further topic from a list of four.

Ordinary level options:
- Further geometry
- Vectors
- Further series
- Linear programming

Higher-level options:
- Further calculus and series
- Further probability and statistics
- Groups
- Further geometry

ASSESSMENT

Leaving Certificate mathematics is assessed by way of a written examination, which examines all topics on the course.

Leaving Cert. Subjects

Geography

The geography syllabus aims to give students the opportunity to develop positive attitudes towards social co-operation, the environment and protection of the world's natural resources. It also aims to develop skills such as map-reading, graph and aerial photograph interpretation and research skills.

The course is divided into core and elective units. Both ordinary and higher level students must study the core units and one of the elective units. Higher-level students must also study one of the optional units.

CORE UNITS

Patterns and processes in the physical environment:

In this unit students study tectonic cycles, rock cycles and landform development. The influence of geological structures and rock characteristics as well as surface processes on landform development is also studied. Students also investigate human interaction and how human activities have impacted on the earth's surface.

Regional geography

This can be broken down into the following topics:

The concept of a region - looking at physical, cultural, socio-economic and climatic regions

Dynamics of a region - how economic, human and physical processes interact in a particular area. Students will look at contrasting regions in Ireland, Europe and the rest of the world.

The complexity of regions – this highlights the interaction between economic, cultural and physical processes and how they affect regions and the EU. It also looks at how boundaries change over time due to urban expansion and EU development.

Geographical investigation and skills

This area teaches skills in handling information and data collection for the completion of a geographical investigation. Students will study map skills, statistics, IT applications etc. They will learn how to plan and structure their investigation and reports, present information and make logical recommendations and conclusions.

ELECTIVE UNITS

Patterns and processes in economic activities

This elective looks at economic development using case studies from developed and developing countries. It also looks at the global economy, patterns in world trade and multinational companies. Students also study Ireland's relationship and membership of the EU and the environmental impact of economic activities.

Patterns and processes in the human environment

This section investigates the dynamics of population such as distribution, growth and structure. It also examines migration and the issues which arise from migration. Students will study different types of settlements and the issues concerned with urban growth.

OPTIONAL UNITS (Higher Level only)

Global interdependence

A study of developed and developing countries, global environmental issues and economic growth. Students also look at the link between human development and future economic development.

Leaving Cert. Subjects

Geoecology

This is the study of soil, soil development and characteristics. It looks at how human interference has made an impact. Students will study world climates and how development and human activity has influenced its change.

Culture and identity

This option investigates populations, their culture, language and religion. It looks at what is meant by nationality and physical and political boundaries. Students will use a case study of a European region and look at their culture, religion, music, migration patterns etc.

The atmosphere – ocean environment

This is the study of the dynamic relationship between the oceans and the atmosphere. Students will study solar energy, oceans, and climatic environments and how they affect economic development.

ASSESSMENT

Leaving Certificate geography is assessed at both ordinary and higher levels. The assessment takes the form of a written examination and a report on the geographical investigation. The written examination is worth 80%. A list of topics for the investigation is published annually and the report is submitted for assessment at the end of the first term in year two of the senior cycle.

Leaving Certificate History

The history syllabus has recently been revised and updated and aims to help students to develop an awareness of human activity in the past from a variety of perspectives. The course studies history in Ireland, Europe and the rest of the world. It also develops a range of research skills and instils an appreciation for historical evidence, helping students to develop an appreciation for the society they live in today.

There are two main elements of the syllabus.

WORKING WITH EVIDENCE:

This section is made up of three parts:

Introduction to history and the historian – this forms the framework for the other parts in this section.

Document based study – the examining authority prescribes a topic each year. The documents to be studied relate to the case studies listed for each topic.

Research study – students choose a topic to investigate and write about it in a report which is submitted for assessment. The report should give an outline plan, an evaluation of the sources and an extended essay.

TOPICS FOR STUDY:

There are two main topics of study:

Early Modern field of study 1492 – 1815.

Later Modern field of study 1815 – 1993.

(Students must select one of these fields of study for examination)

1. Early Modern – 1492 – 1815

This field of study is broken down into sections:
Irish history and the **history of Europe and the wider world**. There are six topics in each section. Students are required to study four topics, two from each section (one of which will have been prescribed as a document based study)

Irish History 1494 – 1815

The topics to be studied in this section are as follows:
- Reform and reformation in Tudor Ireland 1494 – 1558
- Rebellion and conquest in Elizabethan Ireland 1558 – 1603
- Kingdom versus colony – The struggle for mastery in Ireland 1603 – 1660
- Establishing a colonial ascendancy 1660 – 1715
- Colony versus kingdom – tensions in mid 18th century Ireland 1715 – 1770
- The end of the Irish Kingdom and the establishment of the Union 1770 – 1815

History of Europe and the Wider World 1492 – 1815

The topics in this section include:
- Europe from Renaissance to Reformation 1492 – 1567
- Religion and Power – politics in the late sixteenth century 1567 – 1609
- The eclipse of Old Europe 1609 – 1660
- Europe in the age of Louis XIV 1660 – 1715
- Establishing Empires 1715 – 1775
- Empires in revolution 1775 - 1815

2. Later Modern 1815 – 1993

Again, this field of study is broken down into two main sections as above. Students must select two topics from each section.

Irish History 1815 – 1993

The topics in this section are:
- Ireland and the Union 1815 – 1870
- Movements for political and social reform 1870 – 1914
- The pursuit of sovereignty and the impact of partition 1912- 1949
- The Irish Diaspora 1840 – 1966
- Politics and society in Northern Ireland 1949 – 1993
- Government, economy and society in the Republic of Ireland 1949 – 1989

History of Europe and the Wider World 1815 – 1992

The topics to be studied are:
- Nationalism and State formation in Europe 1815 – 1871
- Nation states and international tensions 1871 – 1920
- Dictatorship and democracy 1920 – 1945
- Division and realignment in Europe 1945 – 1992
- European retreat from empire and the aftermath 1945 – 1990
- The United States and the world 1945 – 1989

While the above fields cover a large time span, students are only expected to know the key issues of politics and administration, society and economy, culture, religion and science. Students should also be aware of the key personalities involved.

ASSESSMENT

History is examined at both ordinary and higher levels. Assessment takes the form of a written examination and a research study (20%). Students must complete a report on a selected topic.

Leaving Certificate Modern Languages - French / Spanish / German / Italian

The aim of the French syllabus is to help foster an appreciation for the French language. The language skills learned at Junior Cycle will be built on and developed at Senior Cycle. While this syllabus is specifically discussed in relation to French, the same general framework applies to all modern languages in the Leaving Certificate i.e. Spanish, German and Italian. The main aims of the modern language syllabi are to improve basic communicative proficiency and to make students aware of language and culture.

The syllabus incorporates the following:

Language skills

Students will build on language skills already learned at junior cycle. They will learn the various tenses of verbs (futur, passé compose, conditionnel etc.). Higher-level students will be expected to know compound tenses in addition to the basic tenses. Students will also become familiar with the correct use of adjectives, pronouns and prepositions. All these skills will be tested in the written examination, where the use of correct grammar is essential in obtaining a good grade. Students will also practice speaking French, concentrating on correct pronunciation, vocabulary and the structure of conversations.

Writing skills

This area of the course aims to increase the student's vocabulary and help them to improve writing skills. Ordinary level students will practise cloze tests (filling in the missing words), filling out forms, writing diary entries, message writing and postcards. They will also learn how to compose both formal and informal letters such as applying for a job, asking for information or making a complaint. In addition to this, higher-level students will be expected to be able to write passages about current issues such as unemployment, drug or alcohol abuse, vandalism and smoking. Higher level students will also practise reaction questions, where they are asked to express their view or opinion about a given text or a quote etc.

Comprehension skills

Students will practise comprehension skills by reading passages from books, magazines or past papers and answering questions about the content. Correct usage of grammar and particular tenses is important in this section.

ASSESSMENT

Leaving Certificate modern language is examined at two levels - ordinary and higher. The assessment for both levels takes the same format – an oral, an aural and a written examination. An oral examination will take place prior to the written examination. Students will engage in an informal conversation with an external examiner for about 10 – 15 minutes. The examiner will be looking for pronunciation, vocabulary, structure and communication skills. The oral exam is worth 20% for ordinary level and 25% for higher level. The aural examination which tests listening and comprehension skills will take place on the same day as the written examination. Students will listen to different passages, dialogues etc. and students must answer a series of questions in English. The aural exam is worth 25% for ordinary level and 20% for higher level. The written paper will test students writing, reading and comprehension abilities.

Leaving Certificate Home Economics – Scientific and Social

Home Economics – Scientific and Social continues on from the syllabus at Junior Cycle. It is an applied course that mixes theory with practical skills. It aims to help students develop knowledge, competency and skills for their own personal life and for the environment. It helps them to understand the physical, emotional, economical and social needs of individuals, family and community. There is a common syllabus for all levels with some topics including extra sections for higher-level students. Higher-level students will be expected to demonstrate a greater understanding of concepts and proficiency of skills.

There are three main sections in the core syllabus. There are three elective sections, from which students must choose one.

CORE UNITS

Food Studies

This section includes the following topics:

Food science and nutrition – This is the study of food choices and the properties and functions of proteins, carbohydrates, lipids, vitamins, minerals and water.

Diet and health – Students study dietary requirements and the Irish diet.

Preparation and processing of food – Students learn the importance of food preparation, cooking methods, food safety and hygiene. They also look at the Irish food industry and food legislation

Resource Management and Consumer Studies

The following topics are discussed:

Family resource management – Students learn about human and material resources, needs, wants and the factors that affect management. It also covers household finances and housing.

Consumer studies – a study of consumer choices, responsibility and protection.

The Family in Society

This section highlights sociological concepts such as family structure, marriage and family law.

ELECTIVE UNITS

Home design and management

This involves the provision, design and building of the home, taking into account the family's needs. This elective will be assessed in the final written examination

Textiles fashion and design

This is the study of the design and construction of clothing. For assessment, students will have to design and make a garment that uses a range of prescribed processes.

Social studies

This is a study of the social issues that affect individuals and the family such as unemployment, poverty and education. This elective will be assessed in the final written examination

ASSESSMENT

Assessment is in the form a written examination and practical work. Before the written exam, an external examiner will assess students' practical skills. All elements of the course will be examined in the written exam including two of the elective modules. The Elective module of textile, fashion and design is a practical assessment.

Leaving Certificate Religious Education

The aim of this course is to aid the moral development of students. It will introduce them to ethical codes, they will explore issues of belief and morality in society and it will foster a respect for other beliefs and cultures.

The course is divided into three main units:

UNIT 1

(Students must study all of this unit)

The search for meaning and values

This unit explores the goals and purpose of life and helps students recognise the need to engage in a search for meaning in life as part of personal growth. This unit can be broken down into the following topics:

- The quest for meaning
- The response to the quest
- Concepts of God
- Religion and the emergence of values

UNIT 2

(Students must study 2 topics)

Christianity: Origins and contemporary expressions

This section looks at the origins of Christianity and the formation of the Christian community. It also looks at early Christian movements and compares them to modern day expressions of Christ.

World religions

This area of study develops and encourages respect for the religious beliefs of others and of other cultures. Students will study and compare major world religions and new religious movements.

Moral decision making

This section looks at morality, its principles and theories. Students also look at the link between morality and religion and their own moral development.

UNIT 3

(Students must study one topic from this unit and select two further units from this unit for their coursework)

Religion and gender

This section looks at gender roles in society and religion. Students also investigate the contribution of women in religious traditions.

Issues of justice and peace

This section discusses the links between religious belief and action for justice and peace. It is a social analysis and looks at the religious imperative to act for justice and peace.

Worship, prayer and ritual

This section explores the spiritual dimensions of human life. It looks at symbols, rituals and sacraments, as well as meditation and contemplation.

The Bible: Literature and Sacred Text

This section deals with the literature of the Bible, looking at biblical texts and the link between text and the community.

Religion: The Irish Experience

A look at religion in Ireland, from pre-Christian times to the modern day. It explores the patterns of change and Christianity in Ireland today.

Religion and Science

This topic deals with the relationship between religion and science. Students study current issues for religion and science either in the context of origins or life and death.

ASSESSMENT

This course is examined at both ordinary and higher levels. The students own personal faith or religious affiliation is not subject to assessment. Assessment is a combination of a written examination and coursework. Students must complete an investigation on each of two subjects from unit 3, worth 20% of overall marks. One assignment is done in year one of the leaving certificate and another in year two, but only one piece of coursework is submitted for assessment. The written examination will cover all other elements of the syllabus.

Leaving Certificate Physics

Physics is studied as a separate subject at Senior Cycle, whereas at junior cycle it is a component of the science course, along with chemistry and biology. Students study core topics, options and practical work. While higher-level maths is not required for the study of physics there is a high mathematical content. Students should have a good knowledge of arithmetic, equations and graphs.

The main sections of the course are as follows:

Mechanics:

This involves the study of motion, force and energy.

Temperature:

The concept of temperature, its properties and thermometers are investigated in this section

Heat:

Topics such as heat quantity and how heat is transferred are studied in this section.

Waves:

This section looks at wave frequency, amplitude and the Doppler effect.

Vibrations and Sound:

The speed of sound, its characteristics and vibrations are explored.

Light:

The wave nature of light and colours are studied here. Students also look at lenses, reflection and refraction of light.

Electricity:

This section covers types of charges, electricity conductors and electric fields. Domestic circuits and electromagnetism are also studied.

Modern physics:

This section involves the study of electrons, x-rays and the nucleus. It also covers radioactivity and the study of nuclear energy.

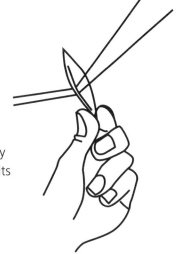

Higher-level students are also required to study one of the following options:

- Particle physics
- Applied electricity

As well as the above core topics, each section also requires students to carry out various types of practical investigations. They must keep a record of all their practical work and retain it for the duration of the course. There are also various equations and formulae which students must know and be able to use.

ASSESSMENT

Assessment is in the form of a written examination. It is examined at both higher and ordinary levels. While both levels use the same core topics, higher-level students must demonstrate a deeper more quantitative understanding of physics.

Leaving Certificate Chemistry

Chemistry at Senior Cycle is studied as a separate subject. The course aims to encourage students' interest in chemistry. It can be treated as a complete course at second level or as a foundation course for further study at third level. As well as studying the theory, students must also complete mandatory experiments and investigations. While there is no requirement for students to study higher-level maths, they should have good arithmetic skills, be competent in carrying out basic calculations and be able to translate information between numerical, graphical and verbal forms.

The course can be divided into the following sections:

Periodic table and atomic structure:

Students will study the elements of the periodic table, the history of atomic structure and radioactivity.

Chemical bonding:

This is the study of chemical compounds, ions and shapes of molecules.

Stoichemistry, formulae and equations:

This section looks at states of matter, gas laws and chemical equations.

Volumetric analysis:

Students look at solutions, acids, and bases as well as carrying out accurate titrations.

Rates of reaction:

Students study the factors that affect rates of reactions and catalysts.

Organic chemistry:

The study of organic compounds and their properties and reaction types.

Fuels and heats of reaction:

The study of hydrocarbons, chemical reactions of temperature and oil refining.

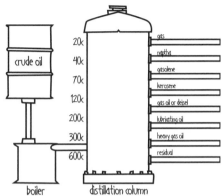

Chemical equilibrium:

Students look at reversible reactions and Le Chateliers Principle.

Environmental chemistry – water:

Students investigate water treatments and analysis. They also look at ph scales and hardness in water.

As well as the above core topics, there are also two options available with two topics in each option. Ordinary level students are required to study only one of the following topics, while higher-level students must study both topics from either option.

OPTION 1:

Additional industrial chemistry:

This involves the study of industrial processes and the characteristics of effective and successful industrial processes, through the use of case studies.

Atmospheric chemistry:

A look at oxygen, nitrogen and carbon dioxide. Students investigate atmospheric pollution and the effects on the ozone layer.

OPTION 2:

Materials:

The study of crystals, metals, alloys and polymers.

Additional electrochemistry and the extraction of metals:

A look at the electrochemical series, electrolysis, corrosion and the manufacture of iron.

ASSESSMENT

All material in the syllabus is subject to assessment. Chemistry is assessed at both ordinary and higher levels and takes the form of a written examination.

Leaving Certificate Biology

At senior cycle biology is studied as a separate subject. The revised syllabus will be examined for the first time in 2004. The aim of the course is to develop students' awareness of biology as a pure science as well as other aspects of biology such as political, social and economic.

The course has three main units:

Biology – the study of life

This unit can be further broken down into the following topics

- The scientific method – a look at the principles and process of experimentation
- The characteristics of life – the definition of life and its characteristics
- Nutrition – the function and chemistry of food
- General principles of ecology – ecology and ecosystems, food chains and pyramids of numbers
- Study of an ecosystem – study of a selected ecosystem, habitats, fieldwork and data collection

The Cell

The topics in this unit include

- Cell structure – a look at plant and animal cells
- Cell continuity – the cell cycle
- Cell metabolism – how cells get energy, enzymes, photosynthesis, respiration
- Cell diversity – a look at tissues, organs
- Genetics – definition of species, genes, DNA, heredity and evolution

The Organism

This unit includes the following topics:

- Diversity of organism – classification of organisms, fungi, bacteria, plant and animal

- Organisation and the vascular structures – flowering plant structures and human circulation

- Transport and nutrition – nutrition in plants and humans, human digestive system and blood transport

- Breathing system and excretion – in both plants and humans

- Responses to stimuli – nerve and sense organ systems, plant responses to stimuli

- Reproduction and growth – plant and human reproductive systems, human development

There are also a set number of experiments and practical investigations that students must carry out and keep a record of throughout their two years of the course.

ASSESSMENT

Assessment is by means of a written examination. Biology is assessed at both higher and ordinary levels. While both levels study the same units, ordinary level students may not be expected to cover certain topics. The ordinary level course provides a broad overview of biology, while the higher-level course provides students with a more in-depth understanding of biology.

Leaving Certificate Technical Drawing

The aim of this course at Leaving Certificate is to provide students with the ability to understand and to present information visually or verbally. It calls on geometric principles to help students solve multi dimensional problems and develops student's spatial perception. It promotes the development of creativity and design ability for the technological world.

The course is divided into two main sections.

Plane and Solid Geometry

This part of the course includes topics such as:

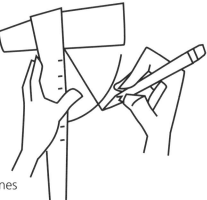

- Scales
- Regular and irregular figures
- Areas of figures
- Projection of solids
- Developments
- Conic sections
- Loci
- The oblique plane
- Surfaces in contact – tangent planes
- Intersections of surfaces or interpenetration of solids
- Pictorial projection

Leaving Cert Subjects

Applications

This section of the course is further divided into two main areas – **engineering and building**.

Building

- Building drawing practice
- Structural forms and concepts
- Building detail
- Building ornament
- Perspective projection
- Shadow projection
- Geometry of shell structures
- Applied geometry in construction technology
- Contouring and applications

Engineering

- Standard specifications and irregular figures
- Engineering components and assemblies
- Fabrication
- Orthographic projection
- Pictorial projection
- Mechanisms
- Drawing office practice.

ASSESSMENT

Technical Drawing at Leaving Certificate is assessed at two levels, ordinary and higher. Assessment is in the form of a written examination, which covers all sections of the course.

Leaving Certificate Business Studies

The aim of this syllabus is to help students prepare for their employment in the business world and also as a basis for further third level studies. The course encourages students to use their own initiative and to develop their enterprise skills. Students will be required to use their knowledge to analyse business information and to provide appropriate courses of action to rectify given business difficulties.

The course can be divided into seven sections as follows:

People in business

This section deals with people and their relationships in business. It examines the conflicting interests among different groups and how these are resolved. Some of the areas dealt with are consumer legislation, trade unions and the small claims court.

Enterprise

This section explains to students the characteristics and skills required to become an entrepreneur. Examples of well-known businessmen will be used to highlight these traits e.g. Richard Branson. The application of enterprise skills in various situations will be analysed e.g. home, school, public service etc.

Management skills

This part of the course distinguishes enterprise from management. The two main leadership styles, democratic and authoritarian will be looked at and the effects of each one compared. Motivation will be covered and McGregor's and Maslow's theories will be looked at in detail. The importance of communication and the different types used will be covered here e.g. reports, letters, graphs etc. The functions of management and structures of organisations will also be looked at.

The applications of management

This section enables students to comprehend how management applies to households and companies. This builds on their knowledge from the Junior Certificate business course and topics such as finance, insurance and taxation are revisited. Students will also learn how to evaluate businesses by applying accounting and ratio analysis. Recruitment and selection procedures are examined in human resource management. Those taking higher level will study business strategies and the concept of total quality management.

Business set-up and expansion

This section looks at the opportunity for starting a business and the roles that marketing and research and development have in it. A key concept here is the marketing mix (the 4P's i.e., price, product, promotion and place). Different types of business require different set up procedures and these will be dealt with. The establishment of a business, sources of finance and business plans are explained. Various methods of expansion such as takeovers and mergers are also explored.

Domestic environment

This section deals with the three types of economic activity: primary, secondary and tertiary. All types of business organisations, from sole traders to multinationals are examined. Community initiatives such as County Enterprise Boards are looked at. Students taking higher level will investigate the relationship between business and the economy and the link between government and business. They will also examine the social responsibility and the code of ethics for businesses.

International environment

The import and export of goods is very significant for Ireland and it can be measured by the Balance of Trade and Balance of Payments. These methods are covered at Junior Cycle but they will be dealt with in greater depth now. The impact of the EU and its policies, e.g. CAP (Common Agricultural Policy) will be analysed. International business is explored in the context of global marketing and transnational companies.

Leaving Cert. Subjects

ASSESSMENT

The Leaving Certificate course is examined at higher and ordinary levels. Assessment is solely based on a written examination. At ordinary level students must answer a combination of short questions (25%) and structured questions (75%). Those doing higher level are required to answer a compulsory Applied Business Question (similar to a case study) worth 20%, short questions worth 20% and the remainder on structured questions.

Leaving Certificate Economics

This course aims to give students an overview and understanding of economic theories and activities. It aims to promote in students the ability to apply economic principles and to relate this information to new situations. Students are encouraged to attain an interest in 'real world' economic activity. This syllabus aims to lead to the pursuit of economics as a course in third level.

The course can be divided as follows:

Introduction

Students learn what economics is and look at basic economic theory.

Production and Consumption

This analyses land, labour, capital and enterprise, as well as production, types of firms and scales of production. The factors that influence industrial location are also discussed e.g. source of raw materials, skilled labour, etc.

Economic Systems and Thought

This explores capitalist to communist economies and contains a rudimentary amount of economic thought. Mixed economies, such as Ireland's are also examined.

Demand and Supply

This examines the concept of a market and it describes the factors affecting demand and supply. Students are required to represent this information graphically and determine points of equilibrium.

Price and Competition

This covers the various market conditions, from monopolies to perfect competition. Students are required to know the characteristics and assumptions of each market type and their effect on supply and demand.

Factor Incomes

A look at the demand for the factors of production and their rewards e.g. rent, wages etc. The effects of trade unions on the equilibrium wage is dealt with and there is a comparison made between the theories of the classical economists and Keynesians.

National Income

Three methods of calculating national income are examined i.e. income, expenditure and output methods. Students learn the importance of its calculation and also its limitations as a measure of economic growth e.g. distribution of wealth. The distinction between GNP and GDP is discussed.

€Exports   € Imports   = €Surplus

Money and Banking

The functions and characteristics of money are covered. Students analyse how the banks create credit and look at various financial institutions e.g. European Central Bank. The factors affecting the supply and demand of money are also discussed.

The Government in the Economy

The sources of Government revenues and expenditures are examined as well as the effects of budget surplus or deficits on the economy. The difference between current and capital expenditure is highlighted here.

Inflation

The causes of inflation are explained and students are required to choose suitable solutions. The consumer price index is studied in detail as well as the various types of inflation. The consequences of inflation are also examined.

International Trade

The advantages and disadvantages of free trade are discussed along with Ireland's participation in the EU. Ricardo's theory of international trade is covered, as well as an investigation of the limitations of free trade.

Terms of Trade

The equilibrium exchange rate is examined and the various rates of exchange are compared. The effects of exchange rates on the Balance of Payments are investigated.

Population

Irish and worldwide population trends are studied as well as the concept of optimum population. The significance of population on economic activity is analysed.

Economic Growth and Development

The importance of economic growth is discussed, especially in relation to Ireland. The advantages and disadvantages of economic growth are analysed.

Economic Policies and Conflicts

Governments have social and economic aims, which are not all attainable. The various policies that government can implement to achieve these goals are explored

ASSESSMENT

Economics is assessed at both ordinary and higher levels. Assessment is in the form of a written examination. While the core syllabus is common for both levels, higher-level students will be expected to prove a greater understanding of concepts and analysis.

Leaving Certificate Accounting

Accounting is a business option at Leaving Certificate. It is a mainly practical subject and helps develop students numeric skills and understanding of business through figures and statistics. It is concerned with the preparation, recording, presentation and analysis of financial information. While it is designed to follow on from business studies at Junior Certificate, it is also designed so that it can be studied without this previous experience.

The course can be divided as follows:

Conceptual framework of Accounting

Students learn the objectives of financial reporting, accounting concepts, bases and policies.

Regulatory framework of Accounting (higher level only)

A study of the regulatory bodies such as government, EU, the accountancy profession and auditors.

Accounting records

Double entry bookkeeping, bank reconciliation statements, control accounts, suspense accounts etc.

Sole traders

Students study the nature and extent of a sole trader and the preparation of trading, profit and loss accounts and balance sheets.

Company accounting

A study of the different types of companies, loan and share capital, financial statements of limited companies and annual reports

Specialised accounts

Students learn about various specialised accounts such as manufacturing, stock, club, service firms, department and farm.

Incomplete records

In this section, students learn how incomplete records arise, and learn how to use control accounts and the net worth method

Cash flow statements

Students learn the importance of cash flow statements and learn to differentiate between profit and cash.

Analysis and interpretation of financial statements

The study of the definition and calculation of accounting ratios and their uses.

Management accounting

Students look at the role of management accounting, cost classifications and budgeting planning and control.

Leaving Cert. Subjects

Information technology and computer applications in accounting

Students learn about the various computer applications and information technology for accounting in a modern business environment.

ASSESSMENT

Leaving Certificate Accountancy is assessed at both higher and ordinary levels. The course content is similar for both levels, although higher-level students have to study a few extra topics. Higher-level students will also be expected to show a greater proficiency in skills, applications and analysis. Both levels are assessed by a written examination.

BULLYING

Bullying

Being a victim of bullying is one of the most distressing experiences for any teenager. Bullying in schools has become the focus for international research for the past twenty years and it is clear that the bullying problem is widespread. Recent studies in Ireland indicate that about 15% of secondary school students are bullied while at school. It's every parents worst nightmare that their child might become involved in bullying as victim or perpetrator; there is however a lot that we as parents can do to prevent it happening and to manage it where it has already occurred / is occurring.

The contents of this article have been drawn from an excellent book entitled **'Bullying in Secondary Schools; what parents need to know'**. It was produced as part of 'The Cool School Programme', an Anti-Bullying initiative for Irish post-primary schools developed within the North Eastern Health Board's Child Psychiatric Services. The book has been written for parents and offers advice on how to prevent and manage bullying, whether your child is a target of bullying, or has a tendency to engage in bullying behaviour.

The book can be ordered by sending a cheque for €10 to: Cool School Programme, Meath Child and Adolescent Mental Health Service, Kennedy Rd, Navan, Co Meath.

Bullying – a definition

The Cool School Programme defines bullying as:

> *'Aggressive behaviour which is an abuse of power by an individual or group against others. It may be physical, verbal or psychological, and is usually deliberate and repeated. Bullying can often be racist, sexual or relational in nature, and those targeted often find it difficult to defend themselves against it'*

Who is likely to become a victim of bullying

Anyone can become a victim of bullying. Even children who do not stand out as being different from others can suffer serious bullying. All it takes is to be in the wrong place at the wrong time. The bully will find something about the child to be the focus of negative attention, or invent a reason. It can happen to anyone.

Certain factors can make children more vulnerable such as

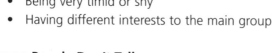

- Physical differences
- Being new to the school or class
- Being adopted
- Recent family stress e.g. bereavement or parental separation
- Needing to wear spectacles or hearing aid.
- Having special needs, e.g. learning difficulties or health problems.
- Being very timid or shy
- Having different interests to the main group

Young People Don't Tell

There is a culture of secrecy surrounding the whole issue of bullying. The fear of retaliation is a legitimate reason not to disclose bullying. There is also the fear of others seeing that you can't cope with the normal cut and thrust of interacting with your peers. Children often decide to put up with bullying rather than confront the possibility of the whole class or school knowing about it. Furthermore, the culture of silence in school is so strong that reporting bullying can be understood to be the same thing as tale telling.

Bystanders who witness bullying often remain silent because they believe it is not their business to intervene. Others may not know how to intervene effectively, or are too afraid to do anything about what they are witnessing. They may be afraid that they will be targeted next. They may have experiences of guilt that they did nothing to stop the bullying.

Bullying

How Can I Know If My Teenager Is Being Bullied?

What makes it difficult for parents to establish whether their teenager is being bullied is that a young person's response to bullying may have similarities to normal adolescent behaviour, caused by stresses other than bullying. For example, being less talkative at home, showing variations in mood, becoming sensitive about appearance, demanding more money and showing signs of being hungry are often part of normal adolescence. The key thing to look out for is sudden and unexplained changes in your child's behaviour. These might include:

Physical signs:
- Unexplained bruising, cuts, scratches, sprains or torn clothing
- Loss of property or damage to personal belongings
- Hunger or thirst due to loss of lunch money to a bully
- Frequent minor illnesses, headaches, stomach aches, nervous rashes, stammering, not eating, bedwetting
- Being obsessive about appearance and cleanliness
- Asking for extra money or stealing (to pay off a bully)

Emotional and psychological signs:
- Fearfulness, acute anxiety, panic attacks
- Avoiding friends and other children
- Uncharacteristic bullying of siblings and/or other students
- Uncharacteristic outbursts of anger
- Refusal to discuss what is wrong
- Change of sleeping or eating pattern
- Becoming withdrawn or moody, dropping usual hobbies and interests
- Loss of confidence or self-esteem
- Excessive tearfulness or crying themselves to sleep, nightmares
- Excessive sensitivity to criticism
- Seeking to be alone
- Implied or overt threats of suicide.

Bullying

Signs related to school:

- Returning from school in a very bad mood and showing reluctance to talk about it
- Unwillingness to go to school or asking to be accompanied
- Changing school route
- Avoiding certain days or lessons
- Uncharacteristic nervousness in class
- Staying close to teachers
- Punctuality problems
- Poor concentration and a deterioration in school work
- Expressions of hopelessness in school work e.g. essays, poems or artwork
- A reduction in phone calls, friends calling, or invitations to social events
- Being excluded from groups
- Not being chosen for sports teams
- A reluctance to take part in previously enjoyed activities
- Abusive phone calls
- Abusive text messages or e-mail.

Is It Bullying?

If you are unsure that your teenager is being bullied or not, considering the following may help you decide:

- Is verbal, psychological or physical aggression being used?
- Is there an imbalance of power because of a wide discrepancy in age, size, strength, or ability to articulate?
- Is the bullying behaviour deliberate?
- Is the person so upset that they feel unable to handle the bullying situation?

What Can I Do If My Teenager Is Being Bullied?

On discovering that bullying is happening you are likely to experience a range of emotions, which may include:

- Anger - you may want to punish the bully
- Helplessness - you may feel there is nothing you can do

- Isolation- you may be unaware of others who have had the same experience
- Confusion - you don't know what to do
- Anxiety - you may be overwhelmed by an instinct to protect your child and find that the problem is all-consuming
- Disappointment - that your child failed to stand up for himself or herself

It is important that you stay calm and avoid over-reacting. Tell your child that you are confident about providing help and support and that you will do whatever is necessary to stop the bullying.

This is a time to show unconditional love and acceptance. Praise your teenager for volunteering the information about the bullying because they have taken the most important step in solving the problem. It is important that they are given whatever time and support is necessary to express their pent-up feelings.

Sometimes parents 'under-react' when a young person tells of being bullied. They may not recognise the significance of the incident for their son/daughter, or the extent to which they have been distressed. Parents need to take bullying seriously, and take steps to support and protect young people, at the earliest possible opportunity.

The following are messages your child needs to hear from you for reassurance:
- 'Bullying can happen to anyone'
- 'It is not your fault'
- 'There is nothing wrong with you'
- 'The bullying should not have happened, and you are not expected to put up with it'
- 'You do not have to face this on your own'
- 'We are going to sort this out'

Safety First

If there has been a physical attack, or threat of one, the school should be contacted before the young person returns to class. Your child should not be encouraged to retaliate, as there may be a risk of injury especially if there is a gang involved. If the incident took place at school, the principal may report it to the police as a matter of policy. You yourself may wish to report the incident to the police, particularly if the assault took place outside the school grounds. Any physical injuries should be treated by a doctor or at a hospital. When considering the young person's safety, you may wish to ask an older brother, sister or friend to keep an eye on them on the way to and from school and within the school itself.

You may wish to advise your child on some of the following things while the matter is ongoing;

- If attacked or in danger, run away and get help
- Stay with a group of friends, and never be last to leave a building or room. There is safety in numbers
- Avoid places where bullying is known to happen, e.g., isolated areas
- Stay in sight of teachers and adults where possible
- Think about varying the times of arrival or departure from school
- Change route to school
- Leave valuable items at home and do not brag about possessions or money
- Do not provoke a bully
- Look the bully in the eye, stand straight and look confident. Stay calm
- Keep a diary of bullying incidents. Record days, dates, times, those involved and what happened
- Shout loudly for help if under physical attack, break free if possible, and run away. Go to the nearest adult for help. Sometimes shouting "NO!" and getting away may be enough to prevent an attack
- If you are cornered and subjected to a physical attack you can try protecting vulnerable parts of the body, especially your head

Fighting Back?

Parents vary in their views on this question. Some believe that the simplest solution is that their child should 'fight back'. Others feel that this should be avoided at all costs. Parents or guardians need to be in agreement about what advice to give to a child in this regard. Lack of consistency leads to confusion for the young person. In reality this is a complex issue with a number of dilemmas, which should be borne in mind. The risk of injury to the child or another person if things go wrong is a serious consideration. Although your teenager may emerge on top from a physical fight, there is no guarantee that he will not be attacked later in revenge, thus escalating the violence. It may be totally unrealistic to expect young people who have been hurt or bullied to fight back. There are other implications also such as disciplinary action from schools, which usually have an absolute ban on fighting.

Fighting back in self-defence may run the risk of being accused of assault. For these reasons the general advice would be that the young person should get away to safety and seek support from a responsible adult. While it is understandable to want to get back at somebody who has hurt you, it would be more constructive to look at ways of stopping the bullying than to cause harm to anyone else.

What to do?

You will need to sit down and discuss with your child how you are going to manage the situation. Explain to them that you may have to contact the school. While there are situations where parents can deal with bullying problems without enlisting the support of the school, this is probably more the exception than the rule.

A young person who is reluctant to tell a teacher for fear of making the situation worse may need to be coaxed. Remember that keeping bullying a secret only allows it to continue. Discuss their worst fears about telling, and assure them you will take whatever steps are necessary to ensure basic safety. If your teenager continues to be adamant, you may need to make a parental decision to override this if their physical well-being or their mental health is compromised. This can be compared with a

Bullying

situation where a child needs urgent medical treatment, e.g., a broken limb. In that instance a parent needs to take control of the situation in the child's best interest.

Approaching The School

Parents are sometimes reluctant to complain to their school about their children being bullied. You may be concerned about how the problem will be handled e.g. will complaining make matters worse. What about confidentiality? Will you be seen merely as a fussy parent or a crank? Will teachers take it as a criticism of their management skills or their professionalism?

While these are understandable concerns, it is important to remember that adult intervention is almost always required to stop bullying when there is an imbalance of power between bully and victim. Because by its nature, bullying happens in secret, you may find that teachers are unaware of the problem. You may also feel impatient if the bullying is not being investigated as fast as you would wish. This might not necessarily mean that the school is dragging its heels. As well as focusing on the needs of your child, teachers may also be interviewing other students and managing the bullying situation within the school's anti-bullying procedures. All this takes time.

School Anti-Bullying Policy

Every school is obliged to have a very specific policy on dealing with bullying. The school's anti-bullying policy should state clearly who your first point of contact should be. Telephone the school and request an appointment with the appropriate person or the Principal.

Bullying

Have your facts prepared:
- Names of children involved and of witnesses. Your son/daughter may not be the only one being bullied
- The nature of the incident/s
- Dates, times and locations of incidents

At the meeting:
- Ask to have the incident investigated.
- Ask what support the school can offer your son/daughter, e.g. counselling or supervised mediation between the parties if appropriate.
- What action will be taken to protect your child from retaliation?

What can you expect from the school
The school's Anti-Bullying Policy Document should clarify the procedures that are in place for dealing with complaints. Most incidents will be dealt with in meetings between the teacher and the accused student(s). Verbal warnings are often sufficient to end the bullying if followed up by frequent monitoring. If the bullying persists or if it is serious enough to warrant it, the parents of the bully may be required to attend a meeting with the principal. In general it is not advisable that you approach the parents of the bully directly.

When the problem has been resolved to your satisfaction and the satisfaction of your child, encourage the young person to go out, make new friends, and avoid brooding. However, he/she will need plenty of encouragement from you at this time to help them come to terms with what has happened. Taking up a new interest or developing a new skill will help your teenager to move on.

Bullying

What Happens If The School Does Not Respond To My Concerns?

Some parents have had the unfortunate experience of having brought bullying to the attention of a teacher or school and yet the bullying persists. It may be that the school is unwilling or does not know how to confront a particularly aggressive pupil. It may be that the nature of the bullying is particularly difficult to address.

If you find yourself faced with a situation where the school claims that they have done all they can to help even though your child is still being bullied, you may have to consider other options.

In some situations you may need to take the problem to the Board of Management or to the Education authorities. In this event it will be important to put all complaints in writing. Address your complaint to the Chairman of the Board of Management, outlining the problem, what steps you have taken so far and what outcome you are seeking. You may be asked to attend a meeting of the Board of Management to discuss the issue. If so, make notes of points you wish to address and keep a written record of the proceedings.

If you are still unhappy with the outcome, you may write to the Divisional Inspector of the area. You will need to find out the name of this official by telephoning the Department of Education & Science.

In rare circumstances you may decide to consider changing schools or alternatively teach the child at home. These are difficult decisions for any parent and you may need to seek advice and guidance from the Department of Education and Science or from education professionals such as the school principal or counsellor. It is important for you as a parent to be sure that a change of school will have the desired result. There are some issues to be considered, particularly the stress that changing school during a school year will put on your already stressed child. Also there is the possibility that your child may not settle well or that she may be bullied again in her new school. Nevertheless there are some children who benefit greatly from a well planned fresh start. If the situation is serious enough to warrant a change of school and you see no other option, then it is important to prepare your son/daughter well for the move.

Stopping bullying before it starts!

There is a great deal that we as parents can do to lessen the likelihood of our teenager being bullied. Confident young people are more likely to stand up for themselves if they are bullied. Building confidence will help your children feel good about themselves and can promote the development of skills to deal with difficult situations. Confidence grows when a child is praised regularly. Remember an ounce of praise is worth a ton of criticism. It is important to be patient with your children and praise them generously for achievements in different areas of their lives.

Parents who communicate with their children on an ongoing basis, will find that they are more likely to discuss difficulties as they arise. There are a few basics that you can put in place, such as ensuring that your son or daughter has basic information on the facts of life so that they do not find themselves ill-prepared for the normal changes of puberty.

Appropriate social behaviour should be taught, e.g. good table manners and personal hygiene. Self-image and physical appearance are very important in adolescence. Teenagers often don't want to appear different from the group and generally want to have the 'in look' which is popular at the time. This may mean that you come under unreasonable pressure to buy expensive brand name clothes and shoes. Without succumbing to this pressure, it should still be possible to allow your child a choice within the budget you can afford.

Bullying

Very shy teenagers

You can help your child develop social skills. Teach your child that being respectful to people does not mean being submissive. Young people can be taught the basic forms of politeness and small talk. They may need  to practise basic greetings in order to open a conversation, e.g., "Hi, do you mind if I sit here? What did you watch on TV last night?" If your son/ daughter is particularly shy, encourage them to watch how other children join in and help them to practise on a one-to-one basis before approaching the group.

A more withdrawn child may need to choose one friendly student to approach first. Children sometimes believe that the established friendships around them are fixed, and closed off to new members, when in reality this may not be the case.

Let them know that it is good to have friends in more than one area of their lives, for instance in their neighbourhood, and in hobby or sports groups, so that if things go wrong in one area, they will have other friends. Hobbies or interest groups, music lessons, dance classes, swimming clubs, self-defence or other one-to-one activities, can pave the way for involvement in wider group activities such as team sports, parties or discos. For quieter children, fan club membership or having a pen-pal, provides an opportunity for one-to-one communication.

Assertiveness

Being assertive means standing up for yourself without being aggressive or apologetic. When it is practised at an early stage before a situation has deteriorated into bullying, it may serve to prevent bullying altogether.

Most bullying begins with some form of verbal comment or aggression, usually name-calling or jeering. A number of techniques can be used either alone or together, which can help a young person deal with difficulties. Practising the following strategies will help young people to use them convincingly. As a parent however, you should be realistic about what your child is capable of doing in a bullying situation. Try to develop confidence by selecting a technique that is manageable and suitable to their capabilities and personality. Emphasise also, that if they find these techniques are not working for them, they should seek additional help from a parent or teacher.

Some assertiveness techniques you can teach your children

"I" Statements
Using brief "I" statements is an effective way to challenge bullying, provided it is used convincingly and with good eye contact. Examples are: 'I don't like your attitude'; 'I don't have to put up with you doing this'; 'I want you to stop hassling me'; 'I don't interfere with you so please leave me alone'.

Here is an example:
'I don't like you calling me names every time I pass by you in the corridor. It annoys me'. Allow time for the other person to respond. You may get an immediate apology because the person involved may not fully realise how hurtful their behaviour has been. If a positive reaction does not emerge, continue with: 'I want the name-calling to stop. If it happens again, I will report it'.

The following points are important to being firm and assertive :
- Know what you want to say
- Say it, concisely and clearly
- Be specific and keep to the point
- Look the person in the eye

Bullying

- Keep calm and relaxed
- Don't laugh nervously
- Be persistent but don't whine

Saying 'No'

If your teenager is being pressured to engage in bullying or other anti-social behaviour, you may need to help them practise saying "No" assertively. Be polite but firm and clear, e.g., "No, I don't want to do that" or "No, I am not getting involved in that". This skill is very necessary when faced with a variety of situations including being offered drugs, drink or unwanted sexual activity.

Broken Record

Broken record means using the same statement over and over again to reinforce a point in a situation where you they feel under pressure to do something you don't want to do e.g. bullying another person. They simply repeat a statement such as:

'I don't want to do this' or
'I don't agree with this' or
'I refuse to be involved here'.

Encourage them to speak politely but firmly. The advantage of this method is that the young person is not making an apology or excuse and does not have to think of clever things to say.

'Fogging'

Fogging is making a neutral comment which conveys the message that the young person has not been bothered by what has been said. For example if the bully makes a nasty personal comment, a fogging response like 'So What!' or Whatever!' or 'I'm not bothered!' might be effective.

If someone responds to a taunt by laughing it off as a first response, it is a sign that the young person can take things in their stride and the bully may give up because they're not getting the negative reaction that they want.

While it is difficult not to take hurtful comments on board, parents can remind their teenagers that a bully who sets out to deliberately hurt and annoy them will be put off if it doesn't appear to be working and they're not getting the desired reaction.

Dealing with abusive text messages

The recent phenomenon of bullying by abusive text messages presents a particular difficulty for parents. Young people are unable to identify the sender (the bully conceals their identity by switching their mobiles into Private Number mode, allowing the abuser to remain anonymous). This allows them to say things that they would never say to a person's face and to send messages at any time and any place. For this reason a victim of this type of bullying is particularly distressed because they cannot escape the bullying and may even be receiving offensive messages during the night.

Because teenagers use their mobile phones as one of the main methods of communication with their peers, it is unrealistic to remove the mobile phones from them. It is important to tell them that they must get help if they are being bullied in this way. Advise your teenager to be very careful about disclosing their phone number. Keep all abusive messages in the phone memory and keep a log of messages. If necessary, change the number and give it only to close family and friends. Young people should be advised to resist the temptation to return offensive messages. If the problem is serious enough it may be a matter for the police.

While mobile phone companies are not the moral guardians of phone users, they will cooperate with the police in tracing blocked mobile numbers used in bullying cases. In Ireland it is an offence in law to send malicious or threatening text messages, covered by the 1999 amendment to the Post Office Act, 1951. If your son/ daughter is receiving threatening or malicious text messages, you should report it to the police.

Bullying

Is my child bullying others?

If you suspect your son or daughter is one of this group, you need to take action because young people who bully are as much in need of support as their victims. Parents can play an important role in helping their children understand the effects of bullying behaviour on others. Students who bully are often not aware of how their behaviour makes others feel. They may get pleasure and a sense of power from bullying. They often believe that bullying will gain them popularity. Young people who tend to bully often have leadership potential, which needs to be channelled in a more positive direction.

Some young people who bully may have been bullied themselves either inside or outside the family. If they are witnessing violence in other areas of their lives they may be imitating it, believing it to be acceptable. Sometimes teenagers may be reacting to family stresses by bullying others. Parents who have a very controlling style while showing little warmth for their children may unwittingly be creating a situation that fosters bullying. Equally, parents who are unclear about rules or boundaries may not be supplying enough support for their children to behave appropriately. Firm, consistent, warm parenting, with good communication is the happy medium

What you can do?

Challenge any aggressive behaviour and insist that it is unacceptable. Explain what is acceptable behaviour and reward it with praise when you notice it. For example, you can discuss how to co-operate with others, ways of asking for things instead of taking them, turn-taking in activities and conversation and so on.

You can establish a basic code of conduct by setting a few important rules at home, e.g. 'treat others with respect', and 'do nothing to hurt yourself, others, or damage property'. Know where your child is at all times, who they are with and what they are doing. Spend time with your son or daughter and talk to them about what is happening in their lives.

Bullying

Is a teacher bullying my child?

If your child complains about a teacher, you need to be able to assess whether the incident is disciplinary in nature or bullying.

You need to take your child seriously if they complain about any of the following: hitting, pushing, being persistently ignored, sexual or verbal abuse, malicious threatening, labelling, ridiculing, insulting, using hurtful sarcasm or fuelling prejudice. Keep in mind however that some anxious children are more vulnerable to a teacher's style of interacting with a class than others. A very timid child may take to heart warnings that are intended for others.

It is very difficult for a parent to approach a teacher with a complaint that they may have bullied their child. It is understandable that you will feel apprehensive about it. Seek an appointment with the teacher concerned and prepare for the interview by writing down the details from your child's point of view. You may wish to have moral support with you for the interview. It will be helpful if you remember that this is not a comfortable situation for a teacher either.

While you are understandably very emotionally involved in representing your child, the problem will be resolved more easily if you can try to keep in mind that the teacher is also a human being, who may or may not have made a mistake in this instance. This stance will make it easier to keep your child's best interests in the foreground of the discussion between yourself and the teacher.

A suggested approach might be: "John is upset and unhappy in class because he feels.... Is there any way we can sort this out together? I would like to hear about it from your point of view" Allow the teacher to explain. Listen carefully without interruption. If the teacher has a reasonable explanation, it is usually possible to solve the problem on the spot.

If you are unhappy with the teacher's explanation, you may wish to seek an appointment with the principal

Bullying

Further Information

As stated at the beginning, the content for this article has been taken from the book 'Bullying in Secondary Schools – What parents need to know', developed by the North Eastern Health Board's **Cool School Programme**.

The Cool School Programme have a great Web Site with links to many other websites on bullying **(www.coolschoobullyfree.ie)**. The book itself contains a lot more information and can be ordered by sending a cheque for €10 to: Cool School Programme, Meath Child and Adolescent Mental Health Service, Kennedy Rd, Navan, Co Meath.

The Department of Education and Science has a document called Guidelines on Countering Bullying Behaviour in Primary and Post Primary (1993). Details on **www.education.ie**

Anti-Bullying Centre, Room 3125, Arts Building, Trinity College, Dublin 2. Phone 01-6082573 (**www.abc.tcd.ie**)

National Parents Council Post Primary: 01-8302740 (**www.edunet.ie/parents**)

Parentline (Parents under stress): 01-8733500 (**www.parentline.ie**)

Bullying

ADOLESCENT DEVELOPMENT

By Dr. David Carey,

Froebel College of Education, Dublin

Adolescent Development

Moody, sullen, oppositional, opinionated, lazy, sleepy; all these and more are among the common terms used to describe teenagers. Parents the world over have been struggling for the last fifty years or more to understand their teenage children. Why do they act the way they do? What happens around age twelve or thirteen to turn that cooperative, pleasant child into a stranger who doesn't seem to want to belong to the family any more? What's going on in there anyway?

An understanding of the adolescent can help us love and cherish them for all the traits that so frequently drive us mad. An adult who takes the time to learn about the tumultuous years of adolescence will soon enough recognise the factors that contributed to their own teenage challenges and will realise that most of what we perceive as troublesome in teens is in fact just the necessary developmental changes they are undergoing on their journey into young adulthood.

A Period of Rapid Change

After infancy the human being will never undergo such a period of growth and development as during adolescence. Everything is growing fast: mind, brain, body and intelligence all experience tremendous change during the teenage years. Unfortunately, unlike infancy, the people around the teenager can't see the struggle for change. We observe our infants and toddlers stumble as they learn to walk, babble as they learn to speak, wobble as they try to run, but we can't observe on the outside the similar changes a teenager is experiencing. Our inability to be witness to the hidden changes of adolescence causes us to puzzle over the external manifestations of this period of great development. When we cannot witness we become anxious and confused. It can be helpful to take the mystery out of adolescence. If we take a look inside and uncover what seems to be deeply hidden we can appreciate the intricacy of adolescent development.

We'll begin our journey with a systematic look at the major areas of change our teens are undergoing. Starting with the psychological movement of adolescence, we will proceed to look at the complexity of the human brain and it's growth during the teen years. We will then look at the influence of familial factors on adolescent growth. We will end our journey with a look at societal factors that further complicate this period of human growth, a period of such great change that it will never be equalled again during the life span.

The Psychology of Adolescence

All human life is movement through social spheres. There is no such thing as an isolated human being. Even the hermit needs a community from which to separate himself. We are born to be social beings and from the very moment of fertilisation we grow in relationship to other people. The struggle to define ourselves as social beings is characterised by our innate need to overcome difficulties and to strive always towards the positive side of life. We will come to look at the social side of the family later in this chapter but for now we must just remind ourselves that all life is movement and take this knowledge to look at the movement of adolescence.

The major task of adolescent psychological movement is to differentiate oneself from the family, to become in their own mind a unique person, not merely an appendage of father, mother, grandparents, and siblings, but a person into oneself. In order to accomplish this necessary task, all sorts of changes must take place. First of all they must have the courage to confront this task. Courage in this sense is strength of heart to begin to venture further from home, to undertake new life challenges such as work, school, sports, and social experiences. In order to manifest this courage it is essential to trust oneself. But the problem is complicated by the fact that in order to trust oneself one has to be willing to make mistakes, learn from them, and have sufficient self-esteem to cope with failure experiences that are inevitable. This requires allies, fellow travellers who they can count on to be there for them, to comfort them in their mistakes, and to encourage them to try again.

The allies the adolescent chooses in the journey to discover the unique self are peers. Who better to accompany them on this rocky road to creating a unique self than others who are travelling along the same path? The peer group becomes so overwhelmingly important during adolescence because it serves as a protecting factor against the family's need to keep the teenager in the nest. The tension between the adolescent striving for independence and the family's unconscious desire to hold on to what is most familiar leads to some interesting events. Any parent of a teenager has experienced some of the amusing, and not so amusing artefacts secondary to the movement for independence.

The family values that were once so solidly embedded in a child suddenly become signposts of rebellion. The teenager won't go to church, believes dad has "sold out" to corporate life, thinks mother is too intrusive, needs to keep secrets, etc. All sorts of contortions begin to occur. Adults puzzle over this, but once we recognise that the peer group and it's seeming magnetic hold on the teen is merely a bridge being used in the journey to creating a new self, we can confront this 'rebellion' in the light of comfort. The comfort comes from the security in knowing that in all but the most extreme cases, the teenagers turn away from family values is temporary. By the time most teens are young adults their core values have returned to those lived by the family. The

rebellion of the teen, articulated by an exaggerated reliance on the peer group, is just an illusion. It is the necessary process of experimenting to discover just who you are and what you believe.

A significant part of the journey to independence is in discovering one's core values rather than merely mimicking them from our parents. Teenagers begin to think deeply about things and this thinking, as we will soon see, is not unlike the act of learning to walk. Although we can't see it, the teenage mind is stumbling from one assumption about life to another, from one moral judgement to another, and it will take a good few years for the mind to sort this out and reach some final, though in themselves fragile, conclusions. Our teenagers are beginning the process of discerning the meaning of life. In childhood the meaning comes from parents and family, in adolescence it begins to come from within. But what is "within" is being created and, as is the case with all creation, various levels of pain and struggle accompany it.

The psychological movement of adolescence is real but hidden from our view. It's helpful to keep in mind this movement and understand that most of what we see on the outside is healthy and necessary for the growth of our teenagers.

The Adolescent Brain

The neurosciences are beginning to unravel the mysteries of the human brain. The grapefruit-sized organ weighing about 2-3 pounds, having the consistency of butter at room temperature is responsible for all we undergo in life. For a long time scientists thought that by middle childhood the brain was nearly fully developed, needing only some small refinement before it reached adult maturity. Recent research is proving this wrong and leading to some interesting discoveries about the adolescent brain.

Adolescence

Our teenagers are a work in progress in more ways than we can see from the outside. The physical changes of puberty take place in the span of a few years but the changes in brain structure, chemistry, and biology take many more years to solidify. That gangly adolescent is even ganglier on the inside, particularly inside the brain.

What part of our brain makes us uniquely human? It's the part on the outer layer, in the frontal lobes of the brain that connect with the inner parts and permit us to manifest what is truly unique about our species. The frontal lobe of the human brain mediates complicated functions such as delay of gratification, ability to tolerate frustration, planning and evaluation of plans, thinking about emotions, controlling of impulses, and learning about life by generalising and drawing conclusions from our mistakes. It is the role of this part of the brain to connect with the deep brain centres, where emotions are generated. In these centres deep inside the brain our emotions are like wild stallions. It is the function of the frontal lobes to put the bridle of reason on emotion.

What relevance does this have to our understanding of the teenager? It has tremendous relevance because we now know that the fibres that connect the frontal lobes to the emotional centres within the brain are not fully mature in early adolescence. In fact, there is mounting evidence that they don't mature fully until early adulthood. If these fibres are not mature, then the mediating functions of the frontal lobes are going to be inefficient in controlling emotion and in making plans, evaluating these plans, and revising them in the light of new data. Although all of the above is oversimplified it does take some of the mystery out of adolescent behaviour. For example, the struggle of so many teens to learn to plan ahead in completing school projects, to understand how to break plans down into manageable units, to revise plans in the light of impending deadlines, all can be seen from the viewpoint of brain development. What may seem like laziness, lack of motivation, and the opposition to study, suddenly becomes comprehensible. There are more teens that have brains undergoing change that will take years to mature than there are 'lazy' kids who don't know the value of education.

Adolescence

Society and the Teenager

Adolescence is a rather recent invention for human beings. For the vast majority of our life on earth there really wasn't adolescence. One simply went from childhood to adulthood. In fact, in many indigenous societies there is no period of adolescence. As the child grows strong and is able to contribute to the community's survival, he or she assumes adult responsibilities. As society has become more complex and legal systems evolved to prohibit child labour, a new view of childhood emerged. This view created a period of preparation for adult life, a period in which children would serve a sort of 'social apprenticeship'. This has evolved into what we now call adolescence. But as society has become more complex, so this process of apprenticeship has become more complex too.

Most adults today have lived in a world of moral surety. There were figures in society invested with tremendous authority. The church, the legal system and our parents and teachers all held moral and physical superiority over us. They told us what to think, what to do, where and when to do it. The consequences of violating these imperatives were swift and sometimes severe. Be it corporal punishment, moral damnation or removal from school, everything in society reinforced the inferior role of the teenager.

No one needs to be reminded that this has all changed. The church has lost its position of authority, school teachers have fallen off their pedestals, parents are no longer dictators in the home, and the result is that the teenager lives today in a world of grey where once they lived through black and white.

Imagine what it is like for our teens today. Undergoing the natural movement towards separation from parents towards individuality, having a brain that is slowly developing, they are living in a world of moral ambiguity with which they are poorly equipped to cope. Even society's over-arching authority, government, is no longer perceived as a source of goodness. Confronted on every side by shades of grey, our teenagers are

Adolescence

increasingly at the mercy of marketing hucksters telling them that significance and individuality come from purchasing the right clothes or most modern mobile phone, and from having a car at age 18!

What is "Normal" Teenage Development?

Adolescence is a period of struggle and growth, most of it happening on the inside. What is visible on the outside is a symptom of an unfolding process of change. It is normal for teenagers to be moody. Most of the mood swings of adolescence are a result of rapid metabolic changes, not emotional turmoil. It is normal for teenagers to be oppositional. What appears as opposition is a testing of the waters of parental love (Do they love me enough to let me be a person on my own rather than an appendage of my parents?). It is normal for adolescents to take extreme moral stances and see the world as morally black and white. This is especially true of the younger adolescent – the brain develops in such a way that subtle moral thinking doesn't usually occur until late adolescence. It is normal for teenagers to become 'infatuated' with a love object. Adolescent love is rehearsal for mature adult love (the bridle of reason must be put on it however). It is normal for the adolescent to turn away from core family values. By young adulthood the family values are usually back in place. It is normal to test adult authority. This is the teenagers attempt to discover how ready they are to face the world on their own.

Adolescence

A lot of what we expect, and what we do to our teenagers is inappropriate. We rush them to make decisions their brains cannot make at too young an age. We expect them to function at levels of maturity that their brains are not able to reach. We use the same methods of discipline at age seventeen we used at age seven, expecting blind compliance from a person engaged in the struggle to become an individual capable of making their own decisions.

Getting it right needn't be so difficult. With a basic understanding of adolescent development we can change the way we think about our teens. When we have changed the way we think, we can accept them for what they are - a work in progress that needs a good bit of trial and error in order to progress. I think it might just help adults if they realise that the toddler who stumbled and fell while learning to walk is hidden inside the adolescent. Stubborn, afraid of being seen as inept, they make mistakes in living and learn from them. Our job as parents of teenagers is to encourage the making of 'better mistakes' and to stand by them with understanding of their development and a deep love of the journey we are on together.

Adolescence

HIDDEN DISABILITIES THAT MAY EMERGE IN SECONDARY SCHOOL

By Dr. David Carey,

Froebel College of Education, Dublin

Hidden Disabilities that may emerge in Secondary School

Statistics indicate that between 7% and 10% of all students in secondary school have a special education need (SEN). The incidence of these needs varies from community to community and is susceptible to variance due to definition, availability of assessment, and terminology. One thing is certain however, a significant number of students in secondary school have special education needs. Educating secondary school students who have a SEN is complicated by a number of factors:

- The age of the child may militate against successful remediation or treatment
- The complexity of the curriculum and the demands of the examination system make it difficult to get academic results of a high quality
- The limited availability of remedial support reduces the opportunities for assistance
- The tendency of some secondary school teachers to be inflexible and unwilling to differentiate their teaching style places the student with a SEN at a disadvantage for learning.

The subject of special education is so wide as to be almost impossible to encapsulate in a short chapter. Because of this the focus of this article will be on the **'hidden disabilities'** that seem to arise when a student moves from primary to secondary school. These hidden disabilities can be a puzzle to parents and teachers alike. They can be just as puzzling to the student who previously had only minor school difficulties but who now finds it increasingly difficult to comprehend material and master content. Although they are hidden they are real, and real special education needs require real solutions.

Hidden Disabilities

What Are Hidden Disabilities?

Primary school is a place where children are provided structure and support; the learning experiences are repeated in a sequence of increasingly complex demands and thoughtful guidance is provided by caring teachers and teaching assistants. Children who struggle and have academic or behavioural difficulties in primary school are usually spotted quickly by their teachers, and reasonably good support systems are currently in place in Irish primary schools. Classroom teachers have been taught how to change their teaching style, methodology and resources (especially the younger generation of teachers). All of this makes it likely that those children with special education needs are recognised early in their primary school years and that appropriate supports are provided.

Despite this there exists a form of special education needs that seem to lie dormant throughout the primary school years, only to manifest themselves during secondary school. Children who appear to be fluent readers suddenly have difficulty comprehending textbook passages. Students who never struggled at mathematics experience problems with calculus, geometry and trigonometry. Attention and concentration, which were once never an issue, suddenly are notably lacking. Memory that was once intact now seems to be faulty. What is happening to change students who were once performing adequately into students who struggle to learn?

The human brain is an organ that grows and develops at its own pace and in a structured, patterned and predictable sequence. The brain is also an organ that is constantly interacting with the external environment. The demands placed upon the brain must match its developmental capacity to meet those demands. Once the demands of the external world exceed the brain's capacity to cope, trouble begins. This is an over-simplified explanation of the term 'hidden disability' but a useful one just the same. For most children the progressively slow pace of the primary curriculum exactly meets their brains ability to cope. The pace of primary school lessons, the number of years being taken to complete primary school, the care and structure provided by primary school teachers all combine to provide an appropriate external environment for the child's brain. Most cope well within this structure.

There are some children, however, whose brains are vulnerable, but not vulnerable enough to bring them to the attention of primary school teachers. The reason for this is the relatively good match between the curricular demands in primary school and the capacity of the child's brain to meet those demands. All things being equal, the curriculum gradually becomes more complex as the brain becomes more capable of handling the increased complexity.

Pace of change and its impact on students

Things can change quite rapidly once the transition to secondary school is made. First of all the pace of lessons accelerates tremendously. The need to prepare for state examinations and the shortness of the school year means that teachers have to compress a huge amount of information into a small number of learning opportunities. The level of comprehension required to read textbooks becomes greater with each passing year of secondary school. The number of textbooks that must be comprehended increases exponentially as well. The demands of the curriculum take an exacting toll on mental capabilities. The number of teachers and the number of teaching styles vastly exceeds whatever was experienced before. It is no wonder, given all the above, that students who never had learning difficulties in the past seem to appear out of nowhere as needing more assistance than any classroom teacher can provide.

This interface between the brain's capacity to learn at different ages and the incredibly complex nature of the secondary school curriculum can overtax the vulnerable brain. When that happens subtle and sometimes not so subtle, learning difficulties become apparent. Though these

Hidden Disabilities

vulnerabilities were present all along, it was the lack of critical demand placed on the brain that caused them to be hidden. The so-called hidden disabilities are real and require intervention. Unfortunately, since they seem to occur out of nowhere parents and teachers often perceive them as laziness, wilful malingering, lack of motivation, or stubbornness. This misinterpretation of real disabilities often results in blaming the student instead of providing support.

The Different Types of Hidden Disabilities

- **Reading Difficulties**
  Many students have difficulty with reading and not all reading difficulties are secondary to hidden disabilities. How can you tell the difference? Well, the surest sign that there is a hidden disability is when it seems to arise out of nowhere, when you haven't been informed during the primary school years that your child may have, or has, a reading difficulty. There might also have been some early indicators of potential reading disabilities such as significant left-right confusion, delayed speech, fine motor or gross motor control problems*, reluctance to draw or colour. But the acid test of a hidden reading disability is its sudden appearance in secondary school. A student may complain of finding the books 'boring', of having difficulty remembering what they have read, or just show signs of being reluctant to read at all when they previously were interested in reading books at home.

- **Mathematical Difficulties**
  The sequential nature of the maths curriculum in primary school, combined with the new emphasis on active learning experiences, makes it difficult to discern which students may have a hidden maths learning disability from those who are reluctant at maths or who have a history of poor teaching of mathematics. In secondary school the maths curriculum becomes increasingly abstract. It escalates in

---

* Fine motor control is the control of small precise movements (pointing to a small item with one finger). Gross motor control is the ability to make large general movements (waving an arm).

complexity at a rapid pace and requires considerable mastery of what was learned before in order to succeed at higher levels of complexity. Students with a history of spatial-perceptual processing (difficulty organising themselves in time and space), may have an underlying processing deficit in the brain that will make higher mathematics problematic. Any sudden, unexplained deficit in maths learning could also be a result of poor teaching so judgement must be suspended until some assessment has been completed.

- **Attention and Concentration Difficulties**
  In secondary school, lessons and the methodology of teaching tend to become centred on lecturing and verbal input. Children who were used to the more experiential mode of learning characterised in the Revised Primary Curriculum have not been accustomed to sitting for long periods of time and listening (at least they aren't supposed to be accustomed to this). As a result, the demands placed upon the 'attentional' systems of the brain were never stressed beyond their functional capacity. Suddenly, and in the space of only two months, the brain has to absorb 40 minutes of verbal input, place it into storage, recall it later, sort it for its essential components, and place it into long-term memory. Students with attentional deficits often come to the attention of teachers and parents during secondary school.

- **Social Difficulties**
  Going through primary school from year to year with the same group of children helps pupils feel secure. They are able to anticipate all possible permutations of behaviour from classmates and know to understand teachers' level of tolerance. Upon entering secondary school everything changes. A new peer group presents new challenges to social affiliation. Up to eight or nine different teachers a day, each with different expectations and different teaching methodologies must be encountered. Although we are programmed by evolution to be social creatures, nothing in our young lives prepares us for the complexity of social interactions we will meet on a daily basis in secondary school.

Hidden Disabilities

- **Emotional and Behavioural Difficulties**
  Unfortunately there are some forms of significant behavioural and emotional disturbances that do not appear until adolescence. There is a form of conduct disturbance, one of the most severe of childhood behavioural disorders, that does not occur until mid-to-late adolescence. The child who previously was cooperative and pleasant seems to turn overnight into an incredibly provocative, rule-violating individual. Some psychiatric disorders do not manifest themselves until adolescence and among the most severe is schizophrenia. Deviant social behaviour under the influence of alcohol or drugs is also a possibility.

What To Do If a Hidden Disability is Suspected

The fatal mistake is to ignore the problem. Any *sudden* change in learning style or proficiency, or a sudden change in behaviour or socialisation is a possible warning sign of a hidden disability. There are, of course, a host of factors that could be causal, including family difficulties, adjustment problems to secondary, a change of housing during adolescence, and death or loss of a loved one. A reasonable guideline is that if a change is noticed and lasts for over three months, it needs to be investigated. Hoping the problem will go away by itself will only lead to further complications and more time needed to treat the problem.

Assessment is the key to discovering whether or not a student has a hidden disability. Assessment must be completed by a professional who has the clinical knowledge to know what to look for and where to look for it. Assessment can be completed by a variety of professionals including qualified special educators, psychologists, speech and language therapists, psychiatrists, paediatricians, (depending on the age of the student) or neurologists. But assessment is only the first step in the process of correcting the problem.

Assessment is only useful if it leads to corrective planning. A diagnosis alone will not deal with a hidden disability. Assessment is a tool to understanding the problem and creating a treatment plan. The plan must be implemented by competent professionals in an educational or clinical setting. It is imperative that all work together in the interest of the student. Isolated interventions are hardly ever successful. Parents must ensure that any assessment will be shared with educators with a view to creating an effective treatment/intervention plan. It is also imperative that parents and educators work together in a spirit of open communication and collaborative planning.

What to Look for In a School

If a student has a hidden disability and assessment has indicated a need for intervention, there are some critical issues that must be confronted in order to proceed. First, the available resources in the school must be scrutinised.

- Does the school have a Learning Support Teacher or a Resource Teacher on the staff?
- If so, how many students are assigned to each caseload?
- What are the maximum number of hours a specialist teacher can provide the student?
- Does the teacher have a higher qualification in special education?
- How willing are subject area teachers to modify their methodology or resources?
- Can structured support for homework be provided?
- What are the attitudes of the teaching staff to the student's difficulties; do they view him or her as lazy and unmotivated as opposed to being a student with a learning difficulty?

What to Look for In Your Family

- Do you, as parents, have an accepting attitude to your child or do you perceive them as lazy and unmotivated?
- Is there an opportunity for you to discuss the problem with the child and come to consensus about the nature of the difficulty?

Hidden Disabilities

- Will siblings be enabled to understand that a genuine problem is present?
- Will the extended family come to the same understanding?
- Can you work cooperatively with teachers and other professionals?
- Are financial resources available to provide private tuition or therapy if necessary?
- Can you, as parents, accept your child as they are without criticism, blame, or guilt?

Conclusion

So-called hidden disabilities are real disabilities. Although they sometimes seem to arise out of nowhere there is often a history of developmental delays and early warning signs. Hidden disabilities can be overcome with proper assessment, treatment, and intervention. This is more likely when all concerned work together cooperatively. An educational environment which is accepting of differing learning styles and learning needs provides the best opportunity for overcoming a hidden disability.

THE UNDERACHIEVING ADOLESCENT

By Dr. David Carey,

Froebel College of Education, Dublin

The Underachieving Adolescent

Why is it that some teenagers perform in school, and sometimes elsewhere in their lives, well below their level of capability? What happens to children when they leave primary school, make the transition to secondary school, and suddenly seem to lose all interest in learning, studying, preparing for exams, and complain that school is "boring"? For many parents the underachieving adolescent is a puzzle and a disappointment at the same time. This chapter takes a look at the factors that lead to underachievement and offers some suggestions about what can be done about it.

Pathways to Failure

The transition from primary to secondary can bring several issues. Primary school tends to be a place where children are structured, nurtured, and looked after. However, secondary school can be a harsh and unforgiving place where an impersonal atmosphere prevails and where high expectations to "get with the programme and plan ahead" are the norm. Many children enter secondary school with a history of poor study habits, poor preparation, and poor planning that primary school teachers have accommodated to some degree. These habits are suddenly no longer tolerated upon entry to secondary school. The pupil, who is not supposed to be a student, is left to his own devices to try and succeed. A significant number of them lack the inner resources to do so.

At the same time the adolescent is struggling to cope with the greater demands of secondary school, he is confronted with the full force of developmental changes of the teenage years, discussed in a previous chapter, see *page 155*. Needing to make educational and career decisions at a young age, an age at which the brain is often unable to cope with these demands, the teenager finds himself caught in a cycle of difficult external demands and undeveloped internal resources. This is a difficult enough process for the average teen but for the underachiever it can become an insurmountable series of obstacles.

Underachievement

The combination of the pressures of adolescent development and the demands of secondary school often produce the classic signs of **underachievement** outlined in Rathvon's book, *The Unmotivated Child*[1], and which include the following:

- Failure to develop meaningful educational and career goals
- Engaging in a pattern of self-defeating behaviour
- Withdrawing from family and friends
- Attachment to an underachieving peer group
- Withdrawal from competitive and evaluative situations
- Feelings of anxiety and depression about the future
- Turing to external sources of gratification (drinking, drugs)

The demands of secondary school can be as tough on the family as they are on the teenager. Faced with the well-founded concerns, and sometimes complaints, from teachers and year-heads, parents become increasingly frustrated with their teenage underachiever, family rows develop, tensions increase in the home, and what was once a loving family becomes a battleground. What is happening inside the teenager to create all these difficulties?

A Look Inside the Mind of the Underachiever

All of us have thoughts, beliefs, and attitudes that were constructed early in life, usually before we had language to describe them to ourselves and to others. These inner "maps" of the outer world consist of images of others and ourselves that are fairly accurate reflections of what we see in the external environment. This inner world of maps and templates are called "working models" of the external world. Most of us have flexible working models and can adjust them as new situations arise. However, for the underachiever the inner world can be a place of rigid demands and badly adapted beliefs. These can persist even when positive

1 Rathvon, N. (1996). The Unmotivated Child. New York: Fireside.

Underachievement

experiences are occurring. It is well known that children reared in stressful environments who have been subjected to harsh corporal punishment, psychological abuse (being told they are stupid, no good, not good enough) often grow up to become underachieving adolescents and adults.

There are many factors that contribute to this type of badly adapted 'working model' of the world and teenagers tend to speak in a sort of coded language. Statements from underachieving children such as, "School is boring", "I'm no good at maths", "The teachers don't care", are all ways of attempting to explain what lies hidden: their working model of themselves and the world. They can however be understood by parents and teachers once we learn how to translate this language into ordinary English.

"It doesn't matter if I study or not. I studied for that exam but failed anyway. I told you, it just doesn't matter!" This statement, heard by many a parent and teacher, is the adolescent's way of telling us they feel as though they have no control over their lives. This feeling of no control is often associated with the state of being highly disorganised. The desks, room or lockers of these teens are more chaotic than those of their peers.

The belief that they have no control of what happens leads them to stop trying to control what happens. The working model of these children prevents them from asking the one thing they most need to ask: "Please help me learn how to control my life, organise myself internally and externally, and to become a successful student."

Teenagers who are chronic underachievers are prone to create catastrophes where none exist. They anticipate failure with exquisite success. They are unable to make the link between preparation and success and therefore believe that nothing matters at all, everything will lead to failure no matter what they do. Having so few inner resources and being dependent on the developmental limitations of the teenage brain, the underachieving adolescent walks through life from one failure to another. These seemingly endless failure experiences have a disastrous effect on self-esteem. Believing that nothing they do leads to success they complicate the matter by *believing* they are failures at school and home. Because our success experiences feed self-esteem, teenagers who have frequent failure experiences learn they are just not up to the task of life, become depressed and feel hopeless. They get bogged down in a cycle of anxiety, failure, damaged self-esteem, more anxiety and more failure. It is a rut that if not interrupted can have disastrous life-long effects.

Turning away help

The underachieving adolescent is caught in another trap: the need for help and assistance and the turning away from it when it is offered. This is an inner dilemma which can be characterised by constant rejection of parent or teacher offers of help. Feeling helpless, inadequate, and lost in a world they cannot comprehend, the underachieving adolescent both wishes for and fears assistance. Indeed, these teenagers can perceive assistance, when it is offered, as some sort of "trick" perpetrated by adults. The underachieving teen has often been reared in a harsh and unforgiving family environment where a belief about innate worthlessness has been unconsciously put into their mind. Given the core belief of being both unloved and unlovable, these teens will quickly perceive any offer of assistance as just another ruse by adults who, they believe, will abandon them at the next failure experience. Why accept help if the helper is only going to insist on instant success?

Unfortunately, the underachieving teenager has such well-entrenched internal beliefs that even success is interpreted as failure. Many teachers and parents have puzzled at the teen that states, after having succeeded in a task at school, "I got lucky, they asked me the things I knew." This

Underachievement

seemingly paradoxical statement must be interpreted for its real meaning, "I'm stupid and unable, and if I succeed it is a matter of luck over which I have no control." The combination of low self-esteem, expectation of failure, the need for help complicated with the rejection of offers of help, all create an exceptionally complex inner working model of a harsh and unforgiving world. The difficulty of parents and teachers to understand this inner world, the harsh and inflexible demands of secondary school and the normal developmental curve of the adolescent brain, all conspire to keep the underachieving teen down at the bottom of the pile.

What happens to the underachieving teenager? Some of them leave school early after a seemingly endless series of failure experiences. Some are encouraged to leave school early by parents and teachers who unwittingly (and sometimes wittingly) send them messages that they don't have what it takes to be an academic success. Some of them, especially those whose working models of the world make them provocative and challenging to the adults around them, are put out of school. Many are just assigned to the scrap heap of teenagers about whom adults have exceptionally low expectations.

The provocative underachiever

A word needs to be said about the provocative and challenging underachiever. Although only a few fit this profile, it is probably the least understood by parents and teachers. What makes a teenager who was once a complaint or cooperative child, become so antagonistic in secondary school? In order to answer this question we must remind ourselves about the working model these teens bring to the external world. The belief that one is unable for the tasks of life, that one is both unloved and loveable, that one can never be a success and that success, when it occurs is a matter of sheer luck, is a combination leading to unpleasant results. These teenagers go through life with a sense of worthlessness that leads them to seek external proof of their internal beliefs. "I am no good and I will prove it to you" is one of the core beliefs of the provocative underachiever. "All adults are unforgiving, pain-inflicting people who will abandon or hurt me, and you are no exception", sums up the inner belief of the provocative adolescent.

These are the teens that "bite the hands that feeds them" and turn against the adults who are trying to help. None of this behaviour is deliberate and wilful. It all stems from the inner world these teens bring to every one and every thing around them.

Helping the Underachieving Adolescent

Becoming an underachieving teenager took a good few years and didn't happen in a week; therefore change will be slow, perhaps laboured and characterised by a bit of back-sliding ('one step forward, two steps back'), **but change and progress can occur**. The goal of change is a "...permanent, positive modification of maladaptive ways of thinking and behaving..."[2]. How long it takes depends in large degree to the adults capacity to support themselves and the teenager as they strive to improve things. Communication between home and school is essential and even more essential is the quality of that communication. Complaints about the underachieving teenager from either side are not helpful or productive. In fact complaints only make matters worse and prove to the underachiever that their working model is in fact correct.

Parents and teachers often mistakenly believe that better grades and academic performance are the first signs of success. In reality social behaviour almost always improves before academic behaviour. This includes a drop in the number of arguments with parents and teachers, a more cheerful and positive attitude, a higher level of energy, increased

2 Rathvon, N. (ibid). p.21

interest in activities that were abandoned previously, and an acceptance of adult feedback, supervision, and positive criticism when it occurs.

What can we, as parents and teachers, do to help?

First of all we must recognise that backsliding is inevitable. Along with this recognition comes the action of never withdrawing support after the first success experience(s). Early withdrawal of support and assistance is a terminal mistake. Remember, no matter what the source of success, the underachiever believes they are a failure. Respond constructively to backsliding; don't panic. Focus on the effort the underachiever is making rather than the product of that effort. Avoid giving bribes and rewards for success. It's the effort that counts and we need to recognise that sustaining effort is difficult for the best of us, incredibly taxing for the underachiever. Have an unshakable belief in the underachiever's ability to overcome their difficulties. Expect improvement over time, not instant results.

Teachers and the underachiever

Teachers have their own unique difficulties with the underachiever. Far too often they take student success as a sign of their own professional expertise and success. In addition, the crushing weight of the curriculum, the demands to generate good examination results, and the pressurised atmosphere of the secondary school, all combine to make it difficult for even the most understanding teacher to be sensitive to the needs of the underachieving student. Waiting for so long for the underachiever to improve can be a frustrating experience. This frustration sometimes leads to the teacher greeting the first signs of change with exasperation or disbelief that it has taken so long to occur. This can undermine the student's commitment to change. The teacher who states, "Will wonders never cease", "I wish you did this a long time ago", or "What took you so long", only make it more difficult for the underachiever to improve. It is especially damaging if such statements are made in front of peers.

Teachers are incredibly influential in the process of changing an underachiever's pattern of behaviour. Like the parents it is important to focus on the effort to change rather than on the results of this efforts.

Underachievement

Taking the time to offer encouragement at even small steps towards improvement is vital. Although it may seem unimportant, and may go unacknowledged by the student, being positive on attitude change or behaviour change is critically important to the student. These teenagers expect adults to be unsupportive and are especially susceptible to even small signs of disapproval. Working cooperatively with parents is also helpful. Taking the time to communicate to the parents when a teacher has observed a change for the better can yield long-term results. Letting parents know when progress is observed, or better still, when effort is being made, is especially helpful. Parents and teachers working together for the good of the underachieving student is the best method of sustaining progress.

Conclusion

The inner world of the underachieving adolescent is a world of low expectations of self and others, of diminished self-esteem, of fear of failure and fear of success, and of a belief that he/she is unlovable and unloved. It is also a world where adults are expected to be unforgiving and pain-inflicting people who say one thing and do another; who deceive you into trusting them only to abandon you when you fail. It is a world of self-fulfilling prophecies that can doom one to a lifetime of struggle, anxiety, and failure. The way out of this maze is not easy or quick. The way out can only be found with the assistance of parents and teachers who refuse to label a person as lazy, stupid, disrespectful, unmotivated, or malingering. For these reasons the lifestyle of the underachieving adolescent can be filled with pain and depression. The stakes are high, the outcome often bleak.

There is no room for loss of hope or removal from school for these teenagers. What is needed is understanding, perseverance and expectations of eventual success. Improvement takes time, sometimes a lot of time, but improvement is a reasonable expectation for the underachieving adolescent.

Underachievement

THE LEAVING CERTIFICATE VOCATIONAL PROGRAMME

The Leaving Certificate Vocational Programme

The Leaving Certificate Vocational Programme was first introduced in 1989, concentrating on three technical subjects and mainly catering for boys. Following the reform and restructuring of the senior cycle, the restructured Leaving Certificate Vocational Programme was introduced in 1994, in response to the challenges placed on the Irish Education system by a changing work and business environment. Students do a minimum of five subjects in the traditional Leaving Certificate (called Leaving Cert. established) and also do two 'Link Modules' in the area of 'Preparation for the world of work' and 'Enterprise Education'. Of the five Leaving Cert subjects, Irish must be included and students must follow a recognised course in a Modern European Language (other than English).

LCVP students follow exactly the same subject syllabi and are assessed in exactly the same way as their peers doing their Leaving Cert. established. The two Link Modules are assessed by way of 'written examination' (40%) and 'Portfolio of Coursework' (60%).

The two Link Modules are treated as one unit for assessment purposes and results in this unit are recognised in points terms by the Universities and Institutes and Technology as follows:

Grade	Percent	Universities and Institutes of Technology award
Distinction	80% - 100%	70 Points
Merit	65% - 79%	50 Points
Pass	50% - 64%	30 Points

The LCVP

In essence, the LCVP combines the academic strengths of the Leaving Certificate (established) with a new and dynamic focus on 'self-directed learning', innovation and enterprise. It's probably best suited to those students who are planning to start their own businesses or seek employment but it's equally relevant to the needs of those preparing for third level education who wish to include a more practical skills-based element to their studies in fifth and sixth year.

'The primary goal of the LCVP is to prepare young people for adult life by ensuring they are educated in the broadest sense, with an ability to cope and thrive in an environment of rapid change'.

Programme Requirements

- At least five Leaving Certificate subjects, one of which must be Irish
- Two of the above subjects must be selected from one of the designated Vocational Subject Groupings (see table below)
- Two Link Modules: Preparation for the World of Work and Enterprise Education
- A recognised course in a Modern European Language other than Irish or English

Vocational Subject Groupings (VSGs)

Two subjects are selected from one of the Vocational Subject Groupings. These subjects provide students with a focus for developing vocational skills and exploring their career options.

The *Specialist Groupings* consist of subjects that complement one another naturally. The *Services Groupings* comprise subjects that complement one another in a commercial context.

Specialist Groupings

1. Construction Studies or Engineering or Technical Drawing (any two)
2. Physics and Construction Studies or Engineering
3. Agricultural Science and Construction Studies or Engineering
4. Agricultural Science and Chemistry or Physics or Physics & Chemistry (combined subject)
5. Home Economics and Agricultural Science or Biology
6. Home Economics and Art
7. Accounting or Business or Economics (any two)
8. Physics and Chemistry
9. Biology and Agricultural Science
10. Biology and Chemistry or Physics or Physics & Chemistry (combined)

Services Groupings

11. Engineering and Business or Accounting or Economics
12. Construction Studies and Business or Accounting or Economics
13. Home Economics and Business or Accounting or Economics
14. Agricultural Science and Business or Accounting or Economics
15. Art and Business or Accounting or Economics
16. Music and Business or Accounting or Economics

The Link Modules

Link Module I - Preparation for the World of Work

- Students will research and investigate local employment opportunities
- Develop job seeking skills such as letter writing, CV presentation, interview techniques
- Gain valuable practical experience of the world of work
- Interview and 'work shadow' a person in a career area that interests them

The LCVP

Link Module II - Enterprise Education
- Students will be involved in organising visits to local businesses and community enterprises
- Meet and interview enterprising people on-site and in the classroom
- Plan and undertake interesting activities that will build self-confidence, creativity, initiative and develop their teamwork, communication and computer skills

Information and Communications Technology
Students taking the LCVP will have an opportunity to develop and apply IT skills. Students should also have an opportunity to use audio/visual equipment and computer presentation packages for recording and presentation purposes.

During the course of the programme students will develop skills to:
- Enter, edit, store, retrieve and print information
- Word process CVs, letters, reports and create illustrated documents
- Send and receive email messages
- Access and use relevant information from CD-Roms and the Internet

Typical LCVP activities include:
- Conducting out of school visits – investigating businesses, community enterprises and other organisations
- Inviting visitors to the classroom other than teachers
- Working in teams on projects and investigations
- Organising 'Enterprise Activities' - setting up projects as vehicles of learning
- Actively preparing for work - career investigation, job search, practise at interviews
- Experiencing the world of work - work experience, work simulation, work shadowing
- Making presentations - to adults and peers
- Using Information and Communications Technology - to access, store, communicate and present information

The Leaving Certificate Vocational Programme

Further Information

Esther Herlihy, Administrative Officer, Navan Education Centre,
Athlumney, Navan, Co. Meath
Phone: 046 9078382
Email: office@lcvp.ie   Website: **www.lcvp.ie**

THE LEAVING
CERTIFICATE
APPLIED

The Leaving Certificate Applied

The Leaving Certificate Applied is a distinct, self-contained two-year programme aimed at preparing students for adult and working life. The programme puts an emphasis on forms of achievement and excellence that the Leaving Certificate (established) has not recognised in the past.

The Leaving Certificate Applied (LCA) was introduced to recognise the talents of all students and provide opportunities for development in terms of responsibility, self-esteem and self-knowledge. The advantage of the LCA is that it focuses on the talents of each individual student and helps students to apply what they learn in the real world.

The unique features of the Leaving Certificate Applied are the curriculum courses involved, the way students learn, the way in which the programme is organised and the way in which students are assessed.

The programme incorporates a common curriculum for all students with a particular weighting on vocational specialisms. The breadth and balance of the curriculum enables the personal development of the student as well as preparation for adult and working life. The curriculum is structured around three main areas.

- **Vocational Preparation** focuses on preparation for work and living, jobsearch skills, work experience, enterprise, community work and English and Communications.
- **Vocational Education** is concerned with the development of mathematical and information communications technology skills and the practical and vocational skills necessary for specialist areas such as hotel catering, engineering, childcare, technology, graphics and construction studies etc.
- **General Education** gives students general life skills including social education, the arts, leisure and languages.

The LCA

A unique feature of the Leaving Certificate Applied curriculum is the fact that Courses in ICT, the arts, leisure and recreation are mandatory for all students and like all Leaving Certificate Applied subjects, are formally assessed in the programme.

The second unique aspect of Leaving Certificate Applied is the way in which students learn. The approach is characterised by educational experiences of an active, practical and student-centred nature. The focus is on the needs and interests of the students, with a strong emphasis on active teaching and learning and using the resources of the local community.

The organisation of the two year programme is also different. First of all the two years is divided into half-year blocks and student learning experiences are planned on the basis of specific requirements, from September to January and from February to June each year. Each course or subject is designed on a modular basis.

With regard to assessment ,Leaving Certificate Applied is assessed in three ways:
- Satisfactory completion of modules
- Student Tasks or projects
- Final Examinations

This assessment is continuous in that it takes place each half year and the students accumulate their credits or marks for their achievement throughout the two years of the programme. A range of modes and techniques of assessment are used in Leaving Certificate Applied including interviews, oral, practical and written examinations.

Students who successfully complete the programme receive a Leaving Certificate from the Department of Education and Science.

This certificate is awarded at three levels based on the total credits which the students have achieved during the two years.

Pass	60-69 %	(120 - 139 credits)
Merit	70-84 %	(140 - 169 credits)
Distinction	85-100 %	(170 - 200 credits)

Further Information
The LCA is available in many schools and centres throughout the country. Details available from:
telephone 061-361993
www.lca.ie
email lca@shanncde.ie

NATIONAL PARENTS COUNCIL POST PRIMARY (NPCPP)

National Parents Council-Post Primary (NPCpp)

The National Parents Council Post Primary (NPCpp) was established in 1985 to act as an umbrella body and forum for its members - established national parents' associations representing the different types of schools operating in the second level sector. These sectors include voluntary, religious, vocational, community and comprehensive.

The parents' association in any state recognised and funded school should be able to affiliate to one of these national parents' associations. Each of these associations have representation on the National Parents Council Post-Primary.

The main objective, for which the Council (NPCpp) is established is: - 'To advance education by involving parents actively in all aspects of the education of their children.'

The Department of Education & Science financially aids the NPCpp and the National Parents Council (Post Primary) Limited is recognised in the Education Act 1998. The Department of Education & Science 'recognises that body (NPCpp) as representing the views of parents in a wide range of fora'. Under the present Memorandum and Articles of Association of National Parents Council (Post Primary) Limited there are five named constituent bodies:

- Federation of Christian Brothers Schools Parents Council (Fed CBS)
- National Congress of Catholic Secondary Schools Parents Association (NCSPA)
- Co-operation of Minority Religions and Protestant Parents Association Post Primary (COMPASS)
- Parents Associations of Community and Comprehensive Schools (PACCS)
- National Parents Association for Vocational Schools and Community Colleges (NPAVSCC)

NPCpp

The Education Act 1998

The Education Act was signed into law on 23 December 1998. It sets out a statutory framework within which the education system can operate and continue to develop. The Education Act places emphasis upon the principle of partnership in the management and operation of the education system. It makes provision for the recognition of schools and the establishment of boards of management in all schools in receipt of public funding. This will ensure that parents, teachers and patrons will have rights under law to be involved in the management of their schools.

The Education Act 1998 placed on a statutory basis for the first time the rights of parents to establish parents' associations in schools and to secure participation on boards of management -:

'The parents of students of a recognised school may establish, and maintain from among their number, a parents' association for that school and membership of that association shall be open to all parents of students of that school'

'The Parents' Association shall promote the interests of the students in a school in co-operation with the board, Principal, teachers and students of a school and for that purpose may-

(a) advise the Principal or the board on any matter relating to the school and the Principal or board, as the case may be, shall have regard to any such advice, and

(b) adopt a programme of activities which will promote the involvement of parents, in consultation with the Principal in the operation of the school

On a practical level, a school's parents' association should be involved in every policy formulation in that school. By law, each school needs an admissions policy and a discipline policy (called code of behaviour).

The Education (Welfare) Act 2000 sets out the 'Code of Behaviour' as follows:

A code of behaviour shall specify-

  (a) the standards of behaviour that shall be observed by each student attending the school
  (b) the measures that may be taken when a student fails or refuses to observe those standards
  (c) the procedures to be followed before a student may be suspended or expelled from the school concerned
  (d) the grounds for removing a suspension imposed in relation to a student
  (e) the procedures to be followed relating to notification of a child's absence from school

Contact Information

National Parents Council Post Primary
Unit 5, Glasnevin Business Centre,
Ballyboggin Road,
Dublin 11.
Tel: +353 (1) 830 2740 / 830 2747
Fax: +353 (1) 830 2752
Email: npcpp@eircom.net
Web: www.npcpp.ie